RENAISSANCE

A HISTORY OF THE

Central West End

Library of Congress Control Number: 2017941019

ISBN: 9781681061245

Written by Candace O'Connor

Design by Richard Roden

Printed in the United States

17 18 19 20 21   5 4 3 2 1

TABLE OF CONTENTS

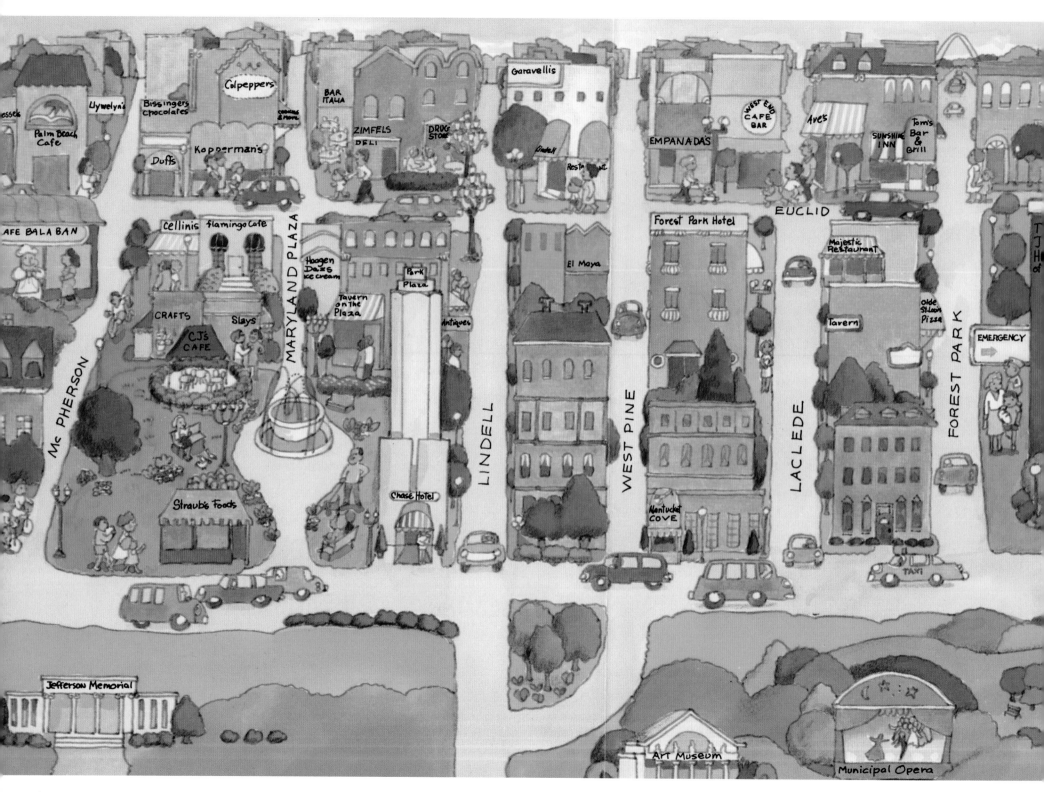

FOREWORD

Francis G. Slay

In this concise but ambitious history of a city neighborhood—St. Louis's renowned Central West End—Candace O'Connor, a St. Louis writer of considerable accomplishment, offers up a complex community fabric, one that reflects elegance, artistry, and resilience, but that also, over time, has been frayed, rended, patiently repaired and restored, and never forsaken.

The history of the Central West End is a history of St. Louis's place in the world. Prior to the completion of Eero Saarinen's stainless steel sculptural masterpiece, the 630-foot-tall catenary arch situated on St. Louis's riverfront, popular imagination of the city may have been most broadly represented by Sally Benson's series of semiautobiographical short stories published in the *New Yorker* magazine.

The stories chronicle St. Louis's Smith family and domestic life during the turn of the twentieth century at 5135 Kensington Avenue—a real St. Louis address situated just a few blocks beyond the Central West End's northern boundary. The Smith family story, culminating in their proud visit to the 1904 World's Fair in their "own backyard," was made into the popular motion picture, *Meet Me in St. Louis.* Amid trolley rides, boys next door, and a merrily melancholy Christmas, the movie memorably depicts picture-perfect homes of grandeur and elegance, surrounded by broad front porches and spacious green lawns, situated on broad, tree-lined streets, in a part of the city that celebrated social prominence and projected virtually unlimited optimism.

This is not mythical imagery manufactured by Hollywood. This is an aspect of life, or at least self-image, in St. Louis's Central West End, a city neighborhood that has had ups and downs and ups from its inception early in the last century to its steady revival over the past forty years.

Ms. O'Connor's history begins and proceeds from the vantage of pedigree and accomplishment of succeeding generations of influential St. Louis families, figures, and institutions, who, over time, built and lived in the Central West End, a magnificent residential district, and developed its internationally preeminent urban park next door—Forest Park. They frequented and supported its cultural institutions, worshipped in its churches, gave talks in its libraries and bookstores, organized social action on its streets and in its sitting rooms, produced literature from rooming houses, reported and editorialized in local journals, tended to the city's ill and made medical breakthroughs in its hospitals, and represented a carriage trade catered to by a succession of fine hotels, shops, and restaurants, as well as a clientele who frequented honkytonks and wrestling matches.

Just as the Smith family story is organized by winter, spring, summer, and fall, the Central West End has gone through many seasons, and not all have been bright. The broader history of the Central West End, like that of the city of which it is a part, for all of the achievement and commitment of many to progress for all, includes heartrending and still unresolved chapters on racism, segregation, poverty, privilege, abandonment, white flight, crime, short-sighted planning, legitimate grievance, and tragic mistrust.

These, too, find expression in Ms. O'Connor's research and prose, in narratives, and in anecdotes.

This history will not satisfy the civic booster or the social critic. It is not an unalloyed celebration or lament, although it has aspects of both. Chapter 5, for example, covers the Central West End today, charting progress from 1975 to the present—notably commenting on work performed in the early 1970s by the planning firm Team Four. This will be sure to generate discussion and, yes, disputation.

These are discussions worth having and are sure to be started by this worthy, accessible contribution to understanding the history of St. Louis and one of its great and historic neighborhoods. ❦

PREFACE

William H. Danforth

Candace O'Connor has written an excellent history of the evolution of the Central West End (CWE) of St. Louis, Missouri. In the early twentieth century, the CWE was an expanding part of its city with clean air, building sites, and a spacious city park. Leading citizens moved into new, attractive homes. Elegant shops followed, as did churches, synagogues, physicians, hospitals, and Washington University's high-quality School of Medicine.

It helps to put the complex politics in context to know that in 1877 St. Louis became a stand-alone city bounded by the Mississippi River and Illinois on the east; the rest is surrounded by, but not part of, St. Louis County, now home to nearly one hundred smaller cities. By the mid-1960s, St. Louis's assets, including physicians, hospitals, and wealth, were leaving the city for surrounding areas.

My involvement began in 1965 when I became vice chancellor for medical affairs of Washington University and president of Washington University Medical School and Associated Hospitals (WUMSAH), an organization designed to coordinate planning and growth. I appointed a committee made up of members from the boards of the WUMSAH institutions, staffed by a talented young physician, Ronald G. Evens, to make recommendations as to how best to deal with three challenges: the movement of medical care to St. Louis County and changes in the neighborhood; the deterioration of the housing stock, with crime and prostitution increasing; and attractive homes for physicians and scientists decreasing. Besides, patients from the county were increasingly reluctant to come to the city for care.

The choices seemed evident:

1) *Stay where we were and work to improve the area.*

2) *Follow other hospitals and move to the surrounding county.*

Ray Wittcoff from the board of Jewish Hospital argued strongly for staying in place, preserving current investments, improving safety, working to strengthen the neighborhood and show loyalty to our home city. Wittcoff's position won the day, and the WUMSAH board, as well as the parent boards, ratified the decision to stay.

After pushback from residents, who had seen drawings of what the area might look like in the distant future, Richard Roloff, soon to join the board of Washington University, met with neighbors and visited house after house to better assess the situation. He worked with planning organizations and then with the board of aldermen, developing understanding and trust.

Later, the board of aldermen voted to use a state law to grant eminent domain to our development organization. Members of Civic Progress, an organization of major companies, agreed to buy bonds paying 6 percent annually to provide the capital to rebuild housing stock. Those investments returned enough to pay off the bonds with full interest.

With the commitment of the medical institutions and visible improvement of their neighborhood, confidence in the property owners of the CWE grew. Others began their own investments and built new institutions and businesses. Eventually, two county hospitals—Missouri Baptist and Christian—joined the group associated with the Washington University Medical School. The new hospital system is named BJC. Charles F. Knight, farseeing chairman of the board of Barnes, was elected first chairman of BJC.

The lesson for many of us was that learning to work together with growing openness, trust, and sense of common purpose resulted in improvement in the region, and that gains spread faster than expected.

The successes in the CWE encouraged us to work together on plant science and, after losing the development of computer technology to the West Coast, on regional economic development. Since 2002, we have developed the area now called Cortex, which has been very successful as a center for innovation. It has strengthened the central spine of St. Louis. Other supportive organizations have also been created. The Coalition for Plant and Life Sciences has evolved into a more effective BioSTL. Progress continues, as do opportunities for more regional groups to work together. The Donald Danforth Plant Science Center was founded in 1998 in St. Louis County in partnership with the Missouri Botanical Garden, Monsanto, the University of Illinois at Urbana-Champaign, the University of Missouri–Columbia, and Washington University. Also, associated commercial organizations have been started close by in St. Louis County. Those stories should soon be ready for telling.

Three final thoughts:

- I have been very fortunate to work with wonderful people: honest, straightforward, unselfish, intelligent, and creative. We have had some impressive accomplishments, none of which a few of us could have done by ourselves.

- I hope that St. Louisans and people from the surrounding Midwest areas will continue to cooperate to improve their home region with concern for what we can do together rather just what I can do with my own piece of turf.

- If we can continue our unselfish entrepreneurial spirit and ability to share visions and work cooperatively toward important goals, I foresee a great future for us all.

JOHN R. LIONBERGER HOME

The John R. Lionberger home at 27 Vandeventer Place was designed by architect H. H. Richardson and built in 1886, undated.

INTRODUCTION

"Comfortable Serenity" —and Back Again

❧

"We are delighted with our new home. Not one of the children laments 3630. David refused to make a visit to the old house, lest some magic should detain him there. Nan is full of hilarity and good spirits. Ruth has a new color in her face. Lutie and I are actually walking in the park. Everything about us is green and lovely. . . . We have taken a new lease of life, and expect to abide a long time in comfortable serenity."

—Isaac Lionberger, resident, in a 1907 letter

"Piece by piece, everything has come back. If you walk along Maryland Plaza at night, people are on the street and in the stores."

—Ellie Chapman, resident, 2016

In 1907, wealthy St. Louis attorney Isaac Lionberger wrote an effusive letter to his sister Mary about the grand, Georgian-style house that he and his wife, the former Louise ("Lutie") Shepley, had just built at 37 Westmoreland Place. Like other affluent St. Louisans, they were moving west, leaving behind their previous home at 3630 Grandel Square off North Grand Avenue, close to the mansion of Lionberger's parents on Vandeventer Place. That once-splendid neighborhood, today the midtown area of St. Louis, was growing shabbier and smokier—so the magnificent private streets near Forest Park, site of the 1904 World's Fair, beckoned irresistibly. As Lionberger told his sister, his wife and children were overjoyed with the change.

Vandeventer Place, 1880

Mary Lionberger, then on a journey to Egypt, must have felt intrigued. Only five years later, after the death of her parents, she moved from Vandeventer Place to her own newly built Tudor Revival mansion at 30 Westmoreland, across the street from her brother. Two Shepley brothers of Louise and a Lionberger nephew also built houses nearby, as did a whole clutch of prominent lawyers, bankers, and businessmen. When Mary died in

Isaac H. Lionberger
(1854–1948)

Vandeventer Place with gates, now in Forest Park, in the foreground, 1885

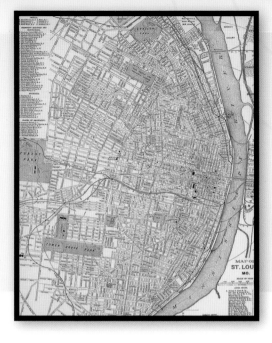

Map of St. Louis, color engraving, 1891. The green areas are local parks.

Panorama of 1904 World's Fair grounds to the northwest, taken from a tethered balloon at nine hundred feet.

1938 at age eighty, she was still living in her Westmoreland mansion. In 1948, Isaac died at ninety-four—and just as he had predicted, he was still enjoying the "comfortable serenity" of his beloved home.

THE GLORY DAYS

When the Lionberger and Shepley clan first moved to Westmoreland Place, the whole area near Forest Park was still basking in the glory of the World's Fair, which had attracted visitors from around the world only a few years earlier. Both before and after the fair, developers raced to build elegant housing in the area known today as the Central West End, which stretches from Delmar Boulevard on the north through Forest Park on the south, and from Sarah on the east to Union Avenue (some say DeBaliviere) on the west. A number of the city's most prominent congregations built sanctuaries in the district; glamorous hotels and a high-end commercial district went up nearby.

Hospitals also joined in this westward march. Robert S. Brookings, president of the Washington University Board of Directors, chose Kingshighway as the new site of the Washington University School of Medicine, formerly in downtown St. Louis. A salesman by profession, Brookings persuaded executors tending the estate of Robert Barnes, a banker who had left his fortune for the founding of a hospital, to establish their

Barnes Hospital, as it appeared in 1915 just after it was completed. The two houses in the foreground were originally segregated wards.

Robert Brookings
(1850–1932)

new "Barnes Hospital" on an adjacent site; he also convinced St. Louis Children's Hospital's board of lady managers to relocate their hospital nearby. Other hospitals also moved into the area: Jewish Hospital, St. John's Mercy, Missouri Baptist, and Shriner's; not far away, Saint Louis University expanded along Grand.

"FROWZY WITH AGE"

But by the time of Isaac Lionberger's death, his street—and indeed the entire Central West End—had lost some of its earlier luster. In the midst of post–World War II era housing shortages, some of the large mansions were being chopped up into small apartments or even rooming houses. Newspapers began to hint ominously at "urban blight" and "property depreciation." Crime began to intrude. A 1956 newspaper story in the *St. Louis Globe-Democrat* described the area as "a dowager . . . grown frowzy with age." Once again, anxious residents began to feel the lure of western suburbs, especially Clayton and Ladue.

By the 1960s and early 1970s, the situation had grown still worse, despite the valiant efforts of residents

The Lindell Hospital in the process of being demolished, undated.

and some developers. High-end retailers fled to the county; so did most of the hospitals, except the Washington University Medical Center. A *Globe-Democrat* story attributed the area's decline, in part, to "an influx of people from the slums cleared out of the Mill Creek area." For the most part, these African American newcomers were not moving to the heart of the neighborhood but rather to the apartment buildings that flanked the area. Still, white flight accelerated. In 1970, said a *St. Louis Post-Dispatch* story, "16 homes on Kingsbury Place were up for sale at one time, and the private streets seemed threatened."

At this point, another family moved to the Central West End with a story very different from the one told years earlier by Isaac Lionberger. They were still drawn to the beauty of the architecture, but the surrounding glory had faded. "There were a lot of vacant houses and a lot of vacant storefronts," recalled Ellie Chapman, who came in 1969 with her husband, William, new rector of Trinity Episcopal Church on Euclid Avenue. Their realtor warned them against the area saying, "Oh, no you don't want to live there!" As Chapman recalls, "we were probably at or near the bottom of the neighborhood's decline. I remember looking around at all the houses: the empty ones, those that were boarded up—or should have been."

Recent photos of the Central West End and Forest Park. *Left*, streetscape; *center*, the World Chess Hall of Fame; *right*, statue of Saint Louis in front of the Saint Louis Art Museum in Forest Park.

Taking a leap of faith, they bought their three-story brick house at 5132 Westminster Place with its six bedrooms and swimming pool out back, all for a bargain price of $24,000. "We saw wonderful housing stock and architecture, and it looked like a really interesting place to live. So we balanced that against the problems and decided to go for it," she adds.

THE CENTRAL WEST END TODAY

Fast-forward through the decades. Today, the Central West End is basking in a new kind of urban glory. Stylish buildings are opening with fine restaurants and high-end merchants. In 2011, the World Chess Hall of Fame set up its headquarters on Maryland Avenue and later hosted the US Chess Championships. "The CWE is currently experiencing the largest residential building boom in St. Louis in decades," boasts the Central West End Association. In 2014, the American Planning Council named the Central West End as one of "10 Great Neighborhoods" in the United States.

Much of the area surrounding the Central West End is also thriving, though the streets north of Delmar remain troubled. On its southern border, Washington University Medical Center—more than 164 acres and 17 city blocks in size—has more than twenty thousand employees and an annual economic impact of $4.4 billion. Forest Park Southeast, with the "Grove" commercial district at its center, has undergone an exciting resurgence. Farther east, the Cortex Innovation Community—a major new bioscience and technology hub, which currently houses some 250 companies—began to develop in 2002, and it is still in the midst of a breathtaking growth spurt.

How did all this happen? In a little more than one hundred years, the Central West End has come full circle: from an area of beautiful neighborhoods, to a

An aerial view of the Washington University Medical Center, 2007

In the Cortex Innovation Community, the Solae/DuPont Headquarters Building, completed in 2010

place in dangerous decline, and now to a diverse and exciting St. Louis showplace. Not all the news is positive; too often, the pleasant street scene is marred by crime. Yet the story of the area's redemption is a remarkable tale of cooperation in which determined residents and business owners worked together with a major institution—the Washington University Medical Center, both its constituent hospitals and its medical school—that simply refused to move. Together, they achieved a kind of miracle of urban rebirth.

Many people—from the leaders of the Medical Center, particularly William Danforth and Raymond Wittcoff; to the developers and urban planners they entrusted with the project, especially Richard Roloff, Jerry King, and Team Four; to the unflinching residents, merchants, religious leaders, and politicians from the neighborhood—have helped to bring about this renaissance. Among the latter group is Ellie Chapman, widowed and remarried, who left her Westminster Place home for an elegant condominium in the Greystone— still in the Central West End. Like Isaac Lionberger, she has never wished to leave. "I really couldn't imagine living any-where else," she says. "Goodness knows, we have the same problems every urban neighborhood has—but this is still a wonderful neighborhood." ❧

PICTORIAL ST. LOUIS

A bird's-eye view of the Central West End, from *Pictorial St. Louis*, Richard Compton and Camille Dry, 1876

CHAPTER 1

A NEIGHBORHOOD OF "LEADING CITIZENS"

The Early Central West End

⚬⚭ (1875–1912) ⚮⚬

"The reader can doubtless think of many leading citizens of whom he would like to know: Where did they come from; where and how were they educated; what is their home life, their religious, social, and political environment…?"

—*The Book of St. Louisans*, 1912

In 1912, the *St. Louis Republic* newspaper published the second edition of its popular volume, *The Book of St. Louisans*, which it had first printed six years earlier. But these weren't just any St. Louisans, still less all St Louisans; no women were featured, nor any minorities. As the subtitle said, this was *A Biographical Dictionary of the Leading Living Men of the City of St. Louis*, and each of these four thousand men got a brief, laudatory write-up that included his address. While they had diverse birthplaces, religions, and professions, these "leading men" were linked by several common threads. All were, or would likely become, rich and powerful. A surprising number had received part of their education—secondary, undergraduate, legal, or medical—at Washington University. And most strikingly, a large percentage of these merchants and lawyers, rabbis and ministers, physicians and academics, bankers and architects, lived in the same magnificent neighborhood: the Central West End.

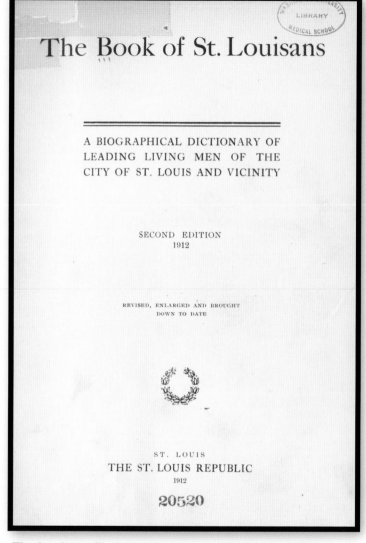

The book profiled prominent men of St. Louis. "The up-to-date merchant, the professional man, the alert inquirer, whatever his vocation, keeps this volume upon his desk, within easy reach," said the foreword.

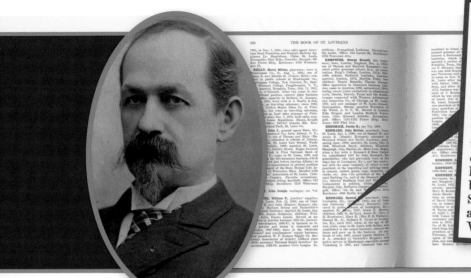

The Book of St. Louisans, published by the *St. Louis Republic* newspaper, first came out in 1906, with a second edition in 1912. "It was recognized at the outset as an invaluable book," said the book's foreword.

There were men like Pierre Chouteau Maffitt of 4315 Westminster and Condé Louis Benoist of 7 Lenox Place, descendants of the fur traders who had founded St. Louis. There were veterans of the Civil War, such as Samuel Kennard who lived at 4 Portland Place, an elegant twenty-five-room house. As board chairman of a leading carpet company, Kennard had fought for the Confederacy, surrendered at Vicksburg to fellow St. Louisan Ulysses S. Grant, and later served as aide-de-camp to Gen. Nathan Bedford Forrest. From the Union side of the war, living at 38 Kingsbury Place, there was John Teasdale, owner of a dried-fruit company, who had enlisted under Gen. Frank P. Blair and was sworn into service by Gen. Nathaniel Lyon. His younger daughter was lyric poet Sara Teasdale.

This billboard advertised the 1904 World's Fair in Minneapolis, Minnesota, 1904.

Many Central West End residents in this book had played a role in the glorious Louisiana Purchase Exposition, known informally as the 1904 World's Fair, held in nearby Forest Park. Chief among them was its president David R. Francis, who had by 1912 served as mayor of St. Louis, governor of Missouri, and secretary of the interior. He lived in a palatial mansion on a five-acre site at 4421 Maryland, where he entertained such fair visitors as US presidents Grover Cleveland, William Howard Taft, and Theodore Roosevelt, as well as Roosevelt's famous daughter Alice Roosevelt Longworth.

David Francis (*left*) and Mark Twain (*right*) standing at the Eugene Field House, 1902

DAVID FRANCIS (1850–1927)

Among all the towering figures in St. Louis during the late nineteenth and early twentieth centuries, David Rowland Francis was surely one of the best known and most powerful. Born in Kentucky, he came to Washington University, graduating in 1870, and he remained in Missouri for the rest of his life. First, he built a successful grain business, but his greatest gift was politics, and he served as mayor from 1885 to 1889 and then governor until 1893. Briefly, he was secretary of the interior under President Grover Cleveland, whom he had ardently supported. Later, he served as ambassador to Russia.

In the late nineteenth century, he became known as a leader of the city's elite—a group widely called the "Big Cinch"—reputed to control commerce in the city and ruthlessly crush opposition. Other Central West End residents in this group included Francis's friend James Campbell of 2 Westmoreland Place, a Civil War veteran on the Union side, who had served on John C. Fremont's staff; and Samuel Kennard of 4 Portland Place, a noted Confederate veteran and first president of the Veiled Prophet (Autumnal Festivities) Association.

But one of Francis's greatest achievements was bringing to life the 1904 World's Fair, which he promoted tirelessly as its president. He recruited his friends to join him in this effort: Campbell was on its executive committee, while Kennard was vice president of the Louisiana Purchase Exposition Co.

When Francis died, US Senator Harry Hawes said of him: "He was a big man who had big conceptions, surrounded himself with big men and did big things. . . . He invited the nation and the nation came; he invited the world and the world came. . . . They visited our city and they liked it. They found it was a city of homes, of generous impulse, of fine old traditions, a place good to live in, to grow up in, and in which to be buried." Like so many of his friends and colleagues, Francis was buried in Bellefontaine Cemetery.

David Francis sitting for a bust sculpted by George Julian Zolnay, 1921–1922

Other residents had played lesser though still important parts in bringing the fair to life. One of the 118 fair directors—Charles Stix, a founder of Stix, Baer and Fuller—lived at 16 Portland Place, while fair treasurer William Thompson, president of the Bank of Commerce, lived at 4487 Lindell. At 14 North Kingshighway was architect George Kessler, who created the master design for the fair site. Louis LaBeaume, another scion of an early French family, lived at 5340 Waterman. Not only had he assisted with fair design, but he had also helped create Second Presbyterian Church at 4501 Westminster Place and in 1912 designed the John F. Shepley home at 53 Portland Place. George Julian Zolnay, a Hungarian American sculptor who lived at 4384 Maryland, was director of the fair's art department.

Many of the men in this volume were businessmen, since St. Louis was then a bustling commercial center—the fourth-largest city in the United States, said the 1910 census—with owners and key officers throughout the Central West End. Edward Faust, second vice president at the growing Anheuser-Busch Brewery, lived at 1 Portland Place. Down the street at number 40 was the home of shoe manufacturer George Warren Brown. This mansion, designed by architect Theodore Link, who also created the gates to the street, featured a Tiffany glass dome in its solarium. Oil merchant James Clark Streett of 4218 Lindell was married to Maud Wells, daughter of the two-term St. Louis mayor and American Steel Foundry Company president, Rolla Wells, who lived doors away at 4228 Lindell. One of the largest homes of all, located at the corner of Lindell and Kingshighway on the site of the later Chase Park Plaza Hotel, belonged to William K. Bixby, retired president of the American Car and Foundry Company.

St. Louis was also a city of religious congregations, several of them fostered or led by Central West End residents listed in this volume. William Thomson of 3805 Lindell helped organize Trinity Episcopal Church on Euclid. Rabbi Samuel Sale, whose home was at 4621 Westminster Place, led Congregation Shaare Emeth for several decades and, said his biographical sketch, "has officiated as chaplain at all national political conventions held in St. Louis." Samuel Niccolls, beloved pastor at Second Presbyterian Church, occupied a manse at 8 Hortense Place. The Irish-born priest Francis Gilfillan, who took charge of the New Cathedral Parish in 1907, lived at 4428 Maryland Avenue.

As other entries showed, eminent physicians lived along Central West End streets. At 5284 Westminster was Washington Fischel, clinical faculty member at Washington University's medical school, which was then preparing to move from downtown St. Louis to a spectacular new Kingshighway campus. Fischel's daughter was suffragist and civic reformer Edna Fischel Gellhorn, who married German-born gynecologist George Gellhorn. Their daughter was Martha Gellhorn, the *Collier's Magazine* correspondent who married Ernest Hemingway. Martha grew up in the neighborhood, learning to dance at Mahler's Ballroom at Euclid and Washington, and attending Mary Institute at Lake and Waterman.

Rabbi Samuel Sale,
1854–1937

Washington Fischel,
1850–1914

Ernest Hemingway Marries a Third St. Louis Girl

THE "ADVENTURESOME" FISCHEL/ GELLHORN FAMILY

In 1940, intrepid young journalist Martha Gellhorn, who had covered the Spanish Civil War, became the third wife of novelist Ernest Hemingway—and all three of the wives had come from St. Louis. Local newspapers were giddy with excitement. The marriage, held in Cheyenne, Wyoming, brought together "two of the most adventuresome spirits in the writing world," said one account.

Martha Gellhorn, whose family home was at 4366 McPherson, also had adventuresome roots. Her mother was Edna Fischel Gellhorn, a respected activist who had fought for women's suffrage, served as the first president of the Missouri League of Women Voters, and later campaigned for a fifty-cents-per-hour minimum wage in Missouri. Martha's father and Edna's husband was George Gellhorn, a respected local obstetrician and gynecologist.

The previous generation was also distinguished. Edna Gellhorn's mother, Martha Ellis Fischel, had directed the St. Louis School of Philanthropy, a predecessor of the George Warren Brown School of Social Work at Washington University. In 1901, she chaired a Wednesday Club committee dedicated to "investigating the condition of women and children employed in factories and stores." Edna's father was Washington Fischel, a prominent internist called by one university chancellor "an eminent physician, a public-spirited citizen, a warm-hearted friend, a noble man." Fischel was also the personal physician of Washington University benefactor Robert Brookings. Like the Gellhorns, the Fischels lived in the Central West End at 5284 Westminster.

The Dwight Davis home was designed by architect James Jamieson, undated.

Finally, as this volume highlighted, Central West End residents included civic leaders. A stellar example was Dwight Davis, 16 Portland Place, a devoted tennis player who had already launched the Davis Cup competition. Trained as a lawyer at Washington University, he became a politician who later served as secretary of war and governor general of the Philippines. In 1912, he was the progressive St. Louis city parks commissioner who encouraged park use, building tennis courts and baseball diamonds. His eventual son-in-law was longtime Federal Reserve chairman William McChesney Martin

**Dwight Davis
(1879–1945)**

Jr., whose banker father was William McChesney Martin Sr. of 422 Lake Avenue.

How did this dazzling assortment of men—along with their wives, families, and servants, as well as the various businesses, schools, and churches that sprang up to serve them—all happen to congregate in the Central West End in 1912? And how did this extraordinary area, filled with architectural beauty and civic accomplishment, develop in the first place?

**William McChesney Martin Sr.
(1874–1955)**

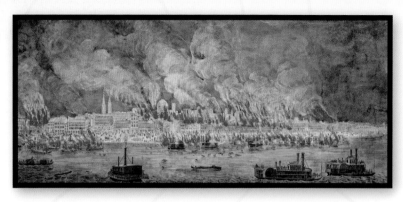

Above, **Great Fire of the City of St. Louis on the 17th and 18th May, 1849.** *Right,* **cholera epidemic of 1873, illustration by J. M. Woodworth, 1875.**

"OH, THIS DIRTY ST. LOUIS!"

From the start, St. Louis had been looking westward. In 1764, Pierre Laclède and his stepson, fourteen-year-old Auguste Chouteau, made the rough, dangerous trip upriver from New Orleans to choose the site for a new trading post and settlement. Some eighteen miles south of the marshy confluence of the Mississippi and Missouri Rivers, they found one: a high spot on the western bank of the Mississippi River, which they named for a king and saint, Louis IX of France. Like Auguste Chouteau and his half-brother Pierre, who became wealthy by trading with the Osage Indians, other early settlers were also fur traders whose territories ranged westward through lands that formed part of the 1803 Louisiana Purchase.

By the 1840s, St. Louis had thriving downtown neighborhoods and a strong business district near the river. But it was dusty and filthy, as Vermont transplant Sarah Smith wrote in 1849 from her new home in the city: "Oh! This dirty St. Louis. There is only one consolation in having so much dirt here. I shall appreciate the cleanliness of Vermont more than I have ever yet done." In that same year came two scourges: a cholera epidemic that killed more than four thousand St. Louisans and a fire on the riverfront that destroyed boats and businesses. "Fire and water seem to be doing what they can to annihilate St. Louis and vicinity," added Smith.

So the population, especially the wealthier citizens, began a pattern of westward relocation that

would recur through coming decades. When the attraction of an old neighborhood waned—as it became too small or less stylish, bordered by noisy businesses, or enveloped in smoke and pollution—people moved west again to the latest fashionable enclave. Starting in 1851, the first stop of some well-to-do St. Louisans fleeing downtown was Lucas Place, the city's first private neighborhood. A fine home on this street, still in existence today as the Campbell House Museum, belonged to fur trader Robert Campbell; the church at the western end of Lucas Place was the now-demolished Second Presbyterian, which would later relocate to the Central West End.

Lithograph of the Lucas Place neighborhood from *Pictorial St. Louis*, by Richard Compton and Camille Dry, 1876

View of Lucas Place, wood engraving, 1860

"If you look at the early history of St. Louis, the well-to-do began moving away from the chaos, noise, and jumble of industry along the river. They moved directly west to get away from it, instead of north and south along the river, and they have done that continuously to this day. There is a kind of 'wealth belt' that comes straight out of downtown, and as they moved west they deposited civic institutions, like the St. Louis Symphony, the Art Museum, and the History Museum. It's called 'place luck.' If you are a neighborhood, it's nice to have place luck. It's nice to have these kinds of urban amenities around you to attract people."

—Todd Swanstrom,
Des Lee Endowed Professor of
Community Collaboration and Public Policy Administration,
University of Missouri–St. Louis

Left, Academic Hall, completed in 1856, was the first building at Washington University. Center, University Hall was built as Collegiate Hall in 1861. Right, Smith Academy began life in Academic Hall but moved in 1879 to a new building at Nineteenth and Washington.

Just north of Lucas Place was the first Washington University campus—its secondary divisions, Smith Academy and Mary Institute; its undergraduate buildings; and its law and medical schools—all clustered near Seventeenth Street and Washington Avenue. Over time, a dingy commercial district, pockmarked by brothels and saloons, grew up around it. When steel-tired wagons bumped noisily over the cobblestones on Washington Avenue and a streetcar line on Eighteenth Street shook the university's science laboratories, research became all but impossible. Smoke coated the windows on the buildings, making the interiors gloomy. As Alexander Langsdorf, an1898 Washington University graduate and later dean of its engineering department, said, "the lighting fixtures [were] so inadequate by modern standards as merely to punctuate the gloom on dark winter afternoons."

Left, 68 Vandeventer Place, Ashley D. and Samuel S. Scott residence, built in 1886. *Center,* East Vandeventer Place gates, c. 1918. *Lower right,* Entrance to Vandeventer Place, c. 1908

Thus, Lucas Place was also uncomfortably close to the heart of St. Louis industrial life, and by the 1870s some affluent St. Louisans began fleeing west to North Grand and the stylish Vandeventer Place designed by Julius Pitzman, later chief engineer in the construction of Forest Park and other private places. This elegant street, one of the finest ever built in the city, included the mansions of David R. Francis, John Lionberger, and oil baron H. Clay Pierce, whose house was said to have cost around $800,000—a breathtaking sum in the late nineteenth century.

JULIUS PITZMAN (1837–1923): MASTER SURVEYOR

The prosperous period spanning the late nineteenth to the early twentieth century was a heyday for homebuilding in St. Louis. Among the owners, architects, and builders who made this boom possible, one name recurs: Julius Pitzman, master surveyor. Quietly, he dominated the construction landscape—in south city, Forest Park, the Central West End, and the Parkview neighborhood—with his fine, detailed designs.

Born in Prussia, he emigrated to the United States in 1858, where he served as a topographical engineer during the Civil War and was wounded at Vicksburg. Next he turned to a career as a surveyor, publishing a respected atlas of St. Louis and laying out many of the area's private streets. In the Central West End, they included Portland, Westmoreland, Kingsbury, and Washington Terrace. He built his own home, No. 6, on Kingsbury Place.

Washington Terrace gate, 1889.

EARLY CENTRAL WEST END HISTORY

Meanwhile, the area that became the Central West End was slowly being discovered. In his *History of St. Louis Neighborhoods,* historian Norbury Wayman traced much of it back to a series of long narrow strips of land, originally French farm tracts. "By the middle of the nineteenth century," he wrote, "most of this land was held by Peter Lindell, William McPherson, and the estate of Nathaniel Pendleton Taylor"—the sources of the present-day Lindell, McPherson, and Taylor street names.

Forest Park was also divided into long east-west strips, he wrote, owned by such descendants of early French landowners as Pierre Chouteau Jr., Jules de Mun, and John Cabanne, as well as Thomas Skinker, Robert Forsyth, and Alban Glasby—most of whom also gave their names to current neighborhood streets. "Cabanne was also the owner of a dairy farm which covered the area now bounded by Lindell, Kingshighway, Delmar, and Union. . . .," wrote Wayman. "During the 1890s, these large tracts were subdivided and those east of Kingshighway were platted for residential uses by the early eighties."

The bird's-eye views of the Central West End published by Richard Compton and Camille Dry in 1876 show an area that had some well-known streets already in place—Lindell, Laclede, McPherson, Union, Kingshighway—but a sparse population. On the northwest corner of Lindell and Taylor was the three-story, mansard-roofed home of Levin H. Baker. At Newstead (then called Cornelia) and Maryland Avenues was the Italianate mansion of Nathan Coleman. Sprinkled along Duncan Avenue, east of Euclid, were country houses and farms. "Across Kingshighway just south of Laclede Avenue was the old John P. Cabanne country home, which was used as a park cottage in 1875," wrote Wayman. "This brick house was the earliest structure built in the area, constructed in 1819 and unjustifiably razed by the park department in 1881." The largest home in the area, at the southwest corner of Kingshighway and Delmar, belonged to George P. Dorris, founder of the Dorris Motor Car Company.

In the early 1870s, the private places that later ran west from Kingshighway, as well as those that ran west from Union Blvd., were still unplatted and even unimagined. The whole section later occupied by Portland and Westmoreland Places was the bucolic Cabanne dairy farm, sold in 1871 to William Griswold, who used it for pasturage. And the site of the Washington Terrace was still the farm of Daniel Bell, whose estate was later subdivided into lots for elegant houses.

"THE GREATEST MONUMENT TO ST. LOUIS"

On June 24, 1876, said the *St. Louis Post-Dispatch* newspaper, crowds began arriving—by carriage, by foot, and by St. Louis, Kansas City & Northern Railroad trains from the Union Depot downtown—in Forest Park for its official dedication. "The Greatest Monument to St. Louis Liberality and Enterprise . . . A Day Long in Memory, First in Pride, and Grandest in Missouri's History . . . One Thousand Acres, Inviting Shades, Handsome Drives, Gorgeous Walks, Limpid Brooks, Dashing Cataracts, and a Profusion of Grandeur Unparalleled," wrote the breathless reporter. "St. Louis Opens to the World," he added, shrinking world geography in his excitement, "the Finest Park on Either Continent."

Forest Park before clearance for the World's Fair, 1901

BEFORE THE WORLD'S FAIR

Forest Park, pedestrian and bridge traffic, c. 1900

Photos of the 1904 World's Fair. *Top left,* View of the Palace of Fine Arts under construction, 1903. *Top right,* Floral Parade of All Nations in the Grand Lagoon in front of Festival Hall. *Middle,* Palace of Agriculture and the Ceylon and Canada buildings. *Bottom left,* Sculpture Hall in the Palace of Fine Arts. *Bottom middle,* crowd of people at St. Louis Day watching a parade. *Bottom right,* Festival Hall and the Central Cascades.

Forest Park sketch class, 1890

Parade down the Pike on the opening day of the horse show at the 1904 World's Fair

A Knights Templar band played rousing selections ("Forest Park Quickstep," "Halloo Balloo Galop"), Governor Charles H. Hardin presided over the ceremony, and Montgomery Blair—a St. Louisan who had served as postmaster general in President Abraham Lincoln's cabinet—gave one of several addresses. A key moment during the afternoon was the unveiling of the twenty-two-foot statue of Edward Bates, attorney general under Lincoln and "one of the most distinguished jurists that ever set foot within the confines of the great City of St. Louis, whose memory, embalmed as it is in the hearts of the nation, is further dedicated today," wrote the same enthusiastic reporter.

The writer cooled down enough to sketch a brief history of the park, around 1,300 acres in size. In 1872, special legislation authorized the purchase of land for a park, but furious landowners contested the bill in court. Two years later, a revised act passed the legislature, allowing the county court to make the purchase. The park was still part of St. Louis County until the 1876 "Great Divorce" of city and county, in which Forest Park joined the city park system. "The price paid," said the reporter, "was nearly $850,000 or about $619.50 per acre" and then added rhapsodically:

"[N]ature had designed that spot for a park. It is neither too rolling for pleasant drives, nor monotonously

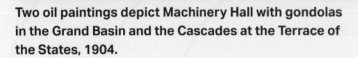
Two oil paintings depict Machinery Hall with gondolas in the Grand Basin and the Cascades at the Terrace of the States, 1904.

level, but comprises the most graceful undulations, gentle slopes, sleeping vales and quiet grottos, relieved by running rills and miniature rivers, besides artificial . . . chains of lakes, in whose limpid waters the silver flash of sporting fish may be seen almost every moment."

From 1875 until the very moment of the dedication, hundreds of workers toiled daily to tame the land, which was marked by remnants of the old dairy farm as well as forests, coal mines, and orchards. The park design came from German-trained landscape architect and park superintendent Maximillian G. Kern, who

would also landscape Westmoreland and Portland Places. He worked with Julius Pitzman, the brilliant chief engineer and surveyor, as well as noted civil engineer Henry Flad. They were assisted by Theodore Link, then a young draftsman but later the talented architect who designed Union Station and a number of Central West End landmarks, including Second Presbyterian Church, St. John's Methodist Church, and new Washington University School of Medicine buildings on its Kingshighway campus.

"At the time of the fair, there were houses along Lindell and a few other blocks of adjacent streets. While most of the private streets had been laid out, they just had a few houses on them. The real development took place right after the fair, starting in 1905. Within ten years, all the big churches had been built along Kingshighway and Union, and the New Cathedral in 1907, along with many other houses as well.

"St. Louis was reaching a kind of heyday in architectural talent when the Central West End was built. To their credit, many of these institutions hired the best architects to build their buildings. Since they were built within a short range of time, you have a lot of continuity in style and materials, and that is one of the things that is so satisfying about this neighborhood. They were also built using very fine materials; because we were a brick-making city then, we have some of the best brick masonry of anyplace in the country."

—Esley Hamilton,
St. Louis architectural historian

BUILDING IN THE LATE-NINETEENTH CENTURY

Not long after the creation of Forest Park, builders began planning elegant new neighborhoods a short distance away. Flush with money from a financial boom in St. Louis—then a manufacturing, beer, bricks, sugar, rail, hardware, tobacco, shoe, and dry goods hub—some of the city's old- and new-money elite were ready to relocate on two of the first streets built: an exclusive, 78-acre development on what used to be the Griswold property, adjacent to the park. A syndicate of investors, the Forest Park Improvement Association, had bought the land for $400,000 in 1887 and hired Pitzman to plan these private places, called Portland and Westmoreland. "The sale of lots in the new subdivision got off to a rather slow start," wrote Julius Hunter in his book, *Westmoreland and Portland Places*, "but by the end of 1897, twenty-nine houses had been erected."

In 1892, J. S. Fullerton began developing a tract he owned on the north side of the Central West End into another exclusive street known as "Fullerton's Westminster Place." Architect W. Albert Swasey, who moved into 4384 Westminster himself, designed its first thirteen houses, which "clearly reflect the sequence of the national trends in style—Romanesque, Italian Renaissance, and Colonial Georgian,"

Entrance gates to Westmoreland Place, c. 1896

HOUSE FOR SALE
FULLERTON'S
WESTMINSTER PLACE

We offer for sale one of the best houses in this beautiful residence place. Near Taylor Avenue; superior construction; house handsomely decorated Fine combination gas and electric fixtures, screens and gas range go with house. Desire to sell at once, and can offer at much less than cost of house, omitting cost of decorating, fixtures, etc. Price and card of admission to interested parties.

ANDERSON-WADE REALTY CO.

Ad from *St. Louis Post-Dispatch*, April 2, 1899

T. S. ELIOT FAMILY HOME

**Home of Henry Ware Eliot,
4446 Westminster, 1917**

Capen Motor Company, 1907

Delmar and Taylor, 1915

wrote architectural historian Charles Savage in his book, *Architecture of the Private Streets of St. Louis*. Then, added Savage, a series of architects from a single firm, Grable & Weber, designed sixteen side-by-side mansions on the street from 1892 to 1902. In 1905, architect Montrose P. McArdle created a red-brick home at 4446 Westminster for Henry Ware Eliot, board chairman of the Hydraulic-Press Brick Company, father of poet Thomas Stearns Eliot, and son of William Greenleaf Eliot, a prominent Unitarian minister and the cofounder of Washington University.

In 1896, Waterman Place was laid out, and the first house on the street—number 41—belonged to Judge James A. Seddon. Other lots went to the family of patent attorney A. C. Fowler. Like other private streets, these houses had the substantial minimum building cost of $7,000. They were also designed by prominent architects, such as W. Albert Swasey. In 1900, George Hellmuth designed a Colonial Revival–style house at 71 Waterman and another at 94 Waterman. Eames & Young designed a house with Craftsman influences at 51 Waterman.

THE SEDDONS OF WATERMAN PLACE

SaLees Smith Seddon

Members of the Seddon family still live in a house on Waterman Place built by their ancestor, Judge James Seddon. One prominent member of the family, committed to civic betterment, was SaLees Smith Seddon, who died in 1984 at age sixty-nine. Her father was attorney Luther Ely Smith, best known as the guiding spirit behind the construction of the Gateway Arch.

His daughter had the same kind of community spirit. In 1959, SaLees Seddon founded the Landmarks Association and later the 1964 Bicentennial Women's Committee, which worked to organize the city's bicentennial celebration. For five years, she was project director of the Women's Crusade against Crime, and in 1973 Gov. Christopher Bond named her the first woman on the St. Louis Police Board.

A 1973 *Post-Dispatch* reporter asked her about urban life. "'Well, I can't imagine why anyone would want to live anywhere but the city,' she said with a laugh. She grew up in a house on Waterman down the block from the house where she and her husband, Dr. John Seddon, now live, and much of her civic activity has been to improve city living."

Luther Ely Smith (1873–1951)

Kingshighway entrance to
Hortense Place, 1940

Still another private street, begun in 1900, was Hortense Place, which had its roots in religious discrimination. Confederate Army veteran and fabulously successful cotton merchant Jacob Goldman wanted to build a mansion in the Central West End, and in the 1890s he tried to buy a lot in the Portland-Westmoreland area. But he was Jewish, and the developers turned him away. Undeterred, he acquired some pasturage along Kingshighway and created his own private place: seventeen elaborate homes, including one for himself designed by architect William Levy, who had also designed the first Jewish Hospital building on Delmar Boulevard. Goldman called the street Hortense Place for his small daughter Hortense, who had died in 1896. A prominent resident at 2 Hortense Place was Albert Bond Lambert, son of the founder of Lambert Pharmaceutical Company, maker of the antiseptic mouthwash Listerine. Lambert, a balloonist, founded an airport in 1920 that grew into Lambert–St. Louis International Airport. He was also a strong backer of Charles Lindbergh in his 1927 transatlantic flight.

Albert Bond Lambert standing on the dedication stone during the 1923 dedication of Lambert Field

GOLDMAN BUILDS HORTENSE PLACE

In 1902, a publication called the *St. Louis Builder* showcased one of the fine new homes going up around the city: the J. D. Goldman mansion on Hortense Place. The title of the article—"Another Beautiful Residence"—hints at how many others were going up at the time. In its lavish descriptions, the story provides a sense of what these extravagant homes looked like, inside and out:

"The house is built of Carthage stone, in the Romanesque style of architecture . . . two stories and an attic, and cost $100,000.

"Modern decoration united with high-class art . . . forms a combination which fills the soul of its possessor with gratitude and joy. Approaching the residence from the south, you enter through a wide vestibule rich in mosaic decoration. The floor and side walls are of marble and the entrance of mahogany with elaborate carvings. . . .

"Going to the rear of this hall, we observe the north main stairs, leading up in two wings to the second floor. On the first landing is observed a very handsome triple art glass window, executed and designed by Emil Frei. This window is an allegorical representation of Art and Peace. The central figure is of a woman representing Peace and bearing in her hand palm branches, surrounded by classical characters. . . .

"Another feature is an electrical light fixture of great brilliancy, novel in its effect and workmanship. This is a stork standing in the water, surrounded by water lilies each forming a bulb for electric lights. The plumage of the stork is formed of prisms of cut glass, within which are different colored electric bulbs, all of which produced when lighted, a luxury of prismatic colors on the foliage made of bronze. . . .

"To the northeast we enter the dining room. This room impresses one with its solid and stately construction of Flemish Green–stained oak, the woodwork being richly carved. . . . The panels in this room are decorated with subjects appropriate for a dining room. . . . Novel and artistic are the decorations in this room, compared with what we usually see. On the ceiling the apple blossom serves as a motive; on the walls different fruit and grapes form the motive, antique gold and red being the predominating color. . . . This room in its whole is art nouveau and a splendid example of modern decoration.

"Last but not least is a ball room . . . with a 15-foot ceiling. The decorations are in pink and cream, and very impressive figures representing dance, with doves and flowers adorning the walls. . . ."

Goldman mansion, 9 Hortense Place,
c. early twentieth century

MOON MOTOR CAR CO.

Moon Motor Car Co., owned by Joseph Moon, 1927

Another exquisite new private street was born in 1892 when Ernest Bell, son of the Daniel Bell who owned the large tract of farmland near Delmar Boulevard and Union Avenue, formed a real estate company and set about developing it. He subdivided the property into fifty lots that averaged an acre in size, with the first two homes constructed in 1895. The 1902 buyer of 5 Washington Terrace was Joseph Moon, proprietor of the Moon Motor Car Company, which had its heyday in the 1910s and '20s. But perhaps the most famous structure on Washington Terrace was its ornate French Norman gatehouse. In 1892, Bell hired a local firm to design the brick tower and clock, and a brilliant but elusive architect at the firm, Harvey Ellis, did the work. Later, the Washington Terrace trustees converted the tower's inside space into living quarters for a part-time custodian.

East entrance of Kingsbury Place, 1890. Note the "Lots for Sale" sign.

In 1902, Kingsbury Place was platted by the omnipresent Pitzman on land formerly owned by sisters Adele and Mary Virginia Kingsbury. This time, Pitzman also built a home on the street, number 6, for himself and his family. Across the street, at number 5, was Washington University plastic surgeon Vilray Blair, famous for his expert head and neck reconstructions. William H. Danforth, founder of the Ralston-Purina Company who espoused a "four-square philosophy of life"— "Stand Tall. Think Tall. Smile Tall. Live Tall."— built an English Tudor–style home at 17 Kingsbury Place. In 1907, Benjamin F. Edwards, principal of the brokerage firm A.G. Edwards, paid $75,000 for an Italian Renaissance–style house at 10 Kingsbury Place.

Finally, investor C. R. H. Davis bought a tract of vacant land east of Hortense Place and developed a small but charming private street, which he called "Lenox Place." Its twenty-seven brick homes, which sold quickly from 1903 to 1905, "are unique," said a 1905 issue of *The Builder*. "They are all of [Davis's] own design and are impressed with his individuality." In January 1904, the *St. Louis Republic* featured a story on No. 3, just sold for $20,000. It had "twelve large rooms, four fine bathrooms, billiard-room, and plenty of closets. The third floor, except billiard-room, is finished in mahogany. . . ."

**Vilray Blair
(1871–1955)**

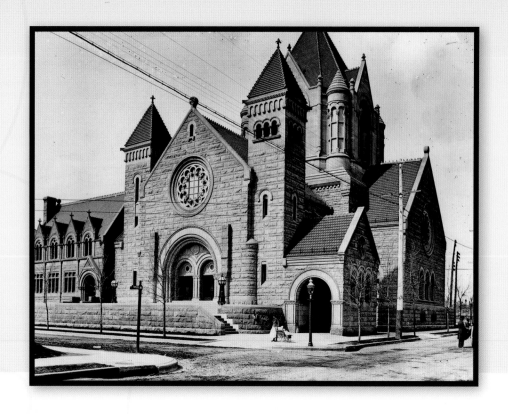

Second Presbyterian
Church, Taylor and
Westminster, undated

CONGREGATIONS CLUSTER IN CENTRAL WEST END

Along with a budding commercial district, churches and synagogues also went up nearby. Second Presbyterian Church at 4501 Westminster Place came early, and it went up in stages: first, the exquisite chapel, designed by Shepley, Rutan and Coolidge in 1896, with a beautiful stenciled-and-beamed ceiling added a little later; next, the Theodore Link–designed sanctuary in 1900 at a cost of $200,000; and finally, an education wing in 1930. The church is still noted for its luminous stained-glass windows, thirteen of which are from the Tiffany Company. One of them, the stunning "Christian Soldier" window in the west transept, is a memorial to soldier Jackson Johnson Jr., who died in World War I. His father, Jackson Johnson Sr., bought the 25 Portland Place mansion of railroad car president William McMillan in 1915. Johnson was the owner of the International Shoe Company, the largest shoe manufacturing company in the world.

Soon after 1900, an entire cluster of buildings—churches, a synagogue, a lodge, and even one private club—was built along Kingshighway, not far from the Delmar intersection. "Holy Corners," as the area was called, included St. John's Methodist, designed by Theodore Link in 1902, at 5000 Washington; First Church of Christ, Scientist, in 1903 at 5000 Westminster, the second building for this congregation, established in 1894; Second Baptist Church, a complex of buildings and bell tower in a Medieval/Renaissance design, constructed in 1907 at 500 North Kingshighway; the colonnaded Temple Israel, 5001 Washington Boulevard, said to be modeled after the Roman Temple of Vespasian; and finally the Tuscan Masonic Temple at 507 North Kingshighway, designed by Albert Groves in the Greek Doric style in 1908.

Left, **North Kingshighway at McPherson, "Holy Corners":** *left to right,* **Tuscan Temple, St. John's Methodist, Temple Israel, 1910.** *Above,* **First Church of Christ, Scientist, undated.**

The Racquet Club, 476 North Kingshighway, 1929

Above, Charles Lindbergh flying over Forest Park, 1927. *Right,* Art Hill crowd watching Lindbergh flyover, 1927.

The private club in the Holy Corners vicinity was the Racquet Club, designed by Mauran, Russell and Garden and founded at 476 North Kingshighway in 1906 as an athletic club for prominent St. Louisans. Later, it played a bit part in international aviation history. In 1927, civic leaders—among them Albert Bond Lambert, a licensed pilot himself and aviation enthusiast; Harry F. Knight, a bond broker living at 4433 Westminster Place; *St. Louis Globe-Democrat* publisher E. Lansing Ray, whose home was at 484 Lake Avenue—met there with Charles Lindbergh and agreed to help fund his historic solo flight across the Atlantic to Paris. Gratefully, he named his plane the *Spirit of St. Louis,* and a replica still hangs from the ceiling of the Jefferson Memorial Building in Forest Park.

All photographs of the Cathedral Basilica under construction, except *second from right*, interior in the 1920s, and *far right*, exterior in 1916

Most spectacular of all the Central West End churches was the Cathedral Basilica, designed by the St. Louis firm of Barnett, Haynes and Barnett, which won a competition for this prized project. The construction of this gigantic building took from 1907 to 1914, and the superb interior mosaic work—nearly 42 million pieces in 7,000 colors, covering 83,000 square feet, with scenes from the Bible and St. Louis life created by twenty different artists—took decades but was finally complete in 1988.

CENTRAL WEST END AUTHORS AND LITERARY SOCIETIES

Not only Sara Teasdale, but also other authors sprang up among the Central West End elite. The family of T. S. Eliot moved to Westminster Place just as Eliot finished Smith Academy and left for Boston, where he would spend a year at Milton Academy and attend Harvard. Next he would move to England—and never live full-time in St. Louis again. But St. Louis lived on in his poetry. In his well-known "Love Song of J. Alfred Prufrock," the Prufrock name may have come from Eliot's dim memory of a downtown furniture store, Prufrock-Litton Company. Eliot's mother, Charlotte Stearns Eliot, was also a poet and author, who wrote a hagiographic biography of her father-in-law, William G. Eliot.

A group of literary women—Charlotte Eliot; Martha Ellis Fischel, mother of Edna Fischel Gellhorn; and others—joined in founding the Wednesday Club, a group that would stimulate their intellectual growth and offer a chance for community service. At first, they had no building of their own, but in 1908 a gift from Lillian Tuttle Bixby, wife of William K. Bixby, allowed them to construct a headquarters building at 4504 Westminster Place,

William Greenleaf Eliot (1811–1887)

T. S. Eliot (1888–1965)

Rev. Samuel Niccolls
(1838–1915)

Theodore Link
(1850–1923)

Kate O'Flaherty Chopin
(1850–1904)

designed by architect Theodore Link. Rev. Samuel Niccolls of Second Presbyterian Church walked across the street to preside at their cornerstone-laying ceremony.

Other writers were beginning to emerge throughout the Central West End. Novelist Kate O'Flaherty Chopin, born in St. Louis, moved back to the city from Louisiana as a widow and mother in 1884. She bought a home at 3317 Morgan, now Delmar, and then she began writing. Like Teasdale, some of her stories appeared in William Marion Reedy's literary journal, *Reedy's Mirror*, and in 1899 she published her sensational novel, *The Awakening*, whose theme of a cheating wife provoked disapproving reviews. The *St. Louis Republic* called it "poison," and even the friendly *Mirror* wished it had never been written. In 1903, Chopin moved to a modest but pleasant home at 4232 McPherson, since named to the National Register of Historic Places, and died in 1904 of a cerebral hemorrhage after visiting the World's Fair.

Below, the Colonnade of States at the 1904 World's Fair. *Top right,* Sylvan Lake, Forest Park, c. 1908. *Second from top,* Hosmer Hall school picnic in Forest Park, c. 1920. *Third from top,* music pagoda in Forest Park. *Bottom right,* automobile in Forest Park, 1908.

FROM "GIANT MONARCHS" TO GIANT PALACES

On April 30, 1904, the Louisiana Purchase Exposition opened with soaring rhetoric from its president, David Francis. ("Open ye gates. Swing wide ye portals.") He would later call the fair "the work of my life." It was a year late but spectacular, with some 1,500 new buildings. Palaces showcased the latest in technology and education, as well as science and art. There were exhibits from fifty foreign nations and forty-three US states, a giant Ferris wheel 265 feet high, and a one-mile "Pike" entertainment strip. By the time it ended seven months later, the fair had attracted some twenty million visitors—opening day alone had drawn two hundred thousand—and transformed the city. In preparation for the fair, city engineers—a number of them Washington University graduates—had finally cleaned up the muddy water supply, builders had thrown up new hotels, and the city had paved dusty streets.

Forest Park, too, was unrecognizable. Thousands of workmen had toiled for months to recreate much of the park: clearing land that had previously been wilderness, especially toward the park's western edge; filling in swamps; re-routing the River des Peres; adding new sewer lines; creating lagoons, pools, and fountains. Altogether, they chopped down some

forty thousand trees, mostly elms and sycamores, and blasted out their stumps with dynamite. "It was a pity . . .," wrote Edward Schneiderhahn, "to see giant monarchs of the forest fall before the woodman's ax to make room for the exhibit palaces."

On the new Washington University campus just west of Skinker Boulevard, the first handful of buildings was leased to fair directors in 1901 as administrative and exhibit space. David Francis's own office was in Room 200 of the building now called Brookings Hall. Next door in Room 220 was a barroom with dirty scratches on the wall from smokers trying to light their matches. Thanks to proceeds from the lease agreement, new buildings—among them, Francis Gymnasium, where the 1904 Olympics were held, and Ridgley Library, where Queen Victoria's Diamond Jubilee gifts were on display—went up on campus. Students at the increasingly shabby downtown buildings were wild with eagerness to move to the new campus, and they hated the delay. "We desire to enter a protest. . . . To divert the buildings to uses entirely foreign to university work . . . we feel would be eminently improper," they wrote before the fair. Still, they had to wait, and the university only moved into its new campus in 1905.

Top left, automobile on Kingshighway, 1906. Center left, skaters in Forest Park, 1907. Bottom left, Forest Park Balloon Race, 1907. Right, sledding on Art Hill, undated.

CULTURAL INSTITUTIONS IN THE PARK

As a legacy of the fair, the park included a number of popular cultural institutions, including a new art museum. Originally, the Saint Louis Museum of Fine Arts was built in downtown St. Louis by Washington University cofounder Wayman Crow as a memorial to his art-loving son, Wayman Jr., who died young. But during the fair, a Cass Gilbert–designed building on a hilltop in Forest Park—one of the few not built of the temporary material called "staff"—became the "Palace of Fine Arts" and afterward it took over as the city's art museum. Briefly, it fell under the aegis of Washington University but then became independent and was renamed the City Art Museum, later the Saint Louis Art Museum.

With money left over from the profitable fair, St. Louis constructed the Jefferson Memorial Building—the first national monument dedicated to President Thomas Jefferson—on the site of the fair's entrance, and in 1913 it became the home of the Missouri Historical Society. This use of the building was fitting, since the Missouri Historical Society had played an important role in attracting and planning the fair. Since then, the museum has become a prominent repository for collections including the area's colonial history, Louisiana Purchase, and Charles Lindbergh, as well as galleries dedicated to the World's Fair.

Wayman Crow (1808–1855)

St. Louis Museum of Fine Arts, the city art museum from 1881 to 1904, at Nineteenth and Locust

Beloved zoo elephant "Miss Jim" surrounded by visitors, 1922

Old Elephant House with visitors, undated

The Saint Louis Zoo was also a beneficiary of the fair. The Smithsonian Institution had commissioned the 1904 Flight Cage for its bird exhibit—then the world's largest aviary—with one thousand birds on display, and they planned to reassemble the cage in Washington, D.C., afterward. But St. Louisans liked it and managed to buy it for the bargain price of $3,500, though it had cost $17,500 to build. The cage became a centerpiece of the new zoo, which officially came into being in 1913 when Mayor Henry Kiel signed a bill giving it seventy-seven acres in Forest Park. Another legacy of the fair was the open-air World's Fair Pavilion on Government Hill in Forest Park. Like the Jefferson Memorial, it was built with funds from the fair and dedicated in 1909.

Left, Olive and Sarah in the early 1900s. *Upper right,* Euclid and McPherson, c. 1910. *Center right,* iconic Central West End street lamp, c. 1910. *Lower right,* Boyle and Lindell, c. 1915.

"DUE WEST"

The fair triggered a building boom in the neighborhoods surrounding a better-groomed Forest Park. North of the park, the Skinker-DeBaliviere neighborhood went up around 1908, while the heart of the Central West End also prospered. "This week closed with . . . the announcement of important building plans in the West End," announced the *St. Louis Post-Dispatch* in November 1910. In the same issue, the Weisels-Gerhart Real Estate Company reported: "The demand for high-class downtown and West End investment property has been one of the features of the fall season." The Blanche Marx house at 5077 Westminster Place sold quickly to William Yantis, vice president of the Norvell-Shapleigh Hardware Company, for $20,000; another at 4347 West Pine with a two-story brick stable went for $13,500. "This company also reports having leased nearly every apartment of the many West End apartment houses under their management," said the newspaper.

In September 1912, the *St. Louis Star* newspaper ran a story, "Two Decades See Values of West St. Louis Multiply," which highlighted "the enhancement in real estate values directly west of the main business center and the millions of dollars that have been expended for building improvements within the past few years out that way. For example: If the

Delmar and Kingshighway, 1910

four corners at Delmar Boulevard and Kingshighway were cleared of their handsome business structures, the vacant spaces would be marketable at $2,500 a front foot. Twenty-five years ago, the same sites were offered at $50 a foot. Kingshighway and Lindell, then worth only $100 a foot, are valued now at $1,500 a foot."

The article continued with other examples of West End growth. "Another citation is the old Cabanne dairy farm. . . . That plot was valued at $2,500 an acre twenty-five years ago. It was purchased, subdivided and sold in the early nineties,

and within fifteen years covered with dwellings that now stand there. . . . Westmoreland and Portland Places were bought for $1,700 an acre; today they are $250 a foot. The ground in these two magnificent places on the northern border of Forest Park has not changed. The location is as it has ever been, but it is the character of the building improvements, and the caste of the people who live there, that has created present values."

Apartment buildings were also rising. In 1907, ads appeared in the newspapers for four "absolutely

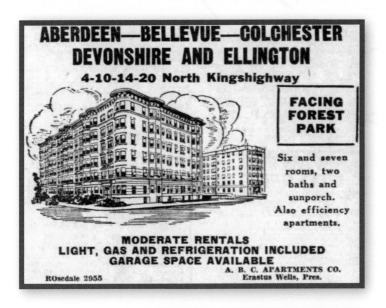

ABERDEEN—BELLEVUE—COLCHESTER
DEVONSHIRE AND ELLINGTON

4-10-14-20 North Kingshighway

FACING FOREST PARK

Six and seven rooms, two baths and sunporch. Also efficiency apartments.

MODERATE RENTALS
LIGHT, GAS AND REFRIGERATION INCLUDED
GARAGE SPACE AVAILABLE

ROsedale 2955

A. B. C. APARTMENTS CO.
Erastus Wells, Pres.

The ABCDE apartments on North Kingshighway, facing Forest Park

fireproof, housekeeping apartment buildings" at 4, 10, 14, and 20 North Kingshighway—the Aberdeen, the Bellevue, the Colchester, and the Devonshire—known familiarly as the "ABC apartments." They called themselves "the first really fine apartment buildings in St. Louis." In 1925, they added the Ellington at Laclede and Forest Park and still later turned into condominiums.

The Central West End was booming, with no break on the horizon. A 1912 article in the *St. Louis Post-Dispatch* confirmed this cheerful assessment. "It is a matter of public knowledge that the better West End properties have in the past five years doubled and trebled in value, and much of it in that period has even exceeded this record." Another story added: "Speculation about the future direction of St. Louis' growth long ago ceased. It is due west. The intensity of present development in the West End affords the alert investor better opportunities than have existed for many years."

It seemed the Central West End would flourish forever. "The expansion, west of this city, has been marvelous, exceeding the predictions of the most optimistic. Imaginary lines mark no boundaries of improvements," continued the story. Added the *Star*, "there is no end to what can be said about the marvelous growth of this great city. . . . The era of prosperity has come to stay."

BARNES HOSPITAL

Barnes Hospital and the Washington University School of Medicine campus, 1931. Note that Kingshighway, later rerouted, is still running alongside the campus.

GLORY DAYS

Splendor amid Hints of Trouble

≈ (1912–1940) ≈

"We have an excellent piece of investment property in the central West End that we can trade for Bank of Commerce stock; this property is a fine income producer, is splendidly located, and is in fine condition; the lady owning it prefers not to be bothered with real estate, so will trade."

—Ad in the *St. Louis Post-Dispatch*, August 4, 1912

J ust south of Westmoreland Place was a parallel line of mansions from 5000 to 5200 Lindell Boulevard—a stretch called Forest Park Terrace—and its houses were as elegant as those on the private streets, since they adhered to the same strict construction standards. One of them was 5125 Lindell, a stately red-brick, colonnaded mansion designed by Eames & Young, and in 1899 it became the home of forty-nine-year-old Robert Brookings, who had first made a fortune in business and then turned to a philanthropic pursuit: saving Washington University. At the end of the nineteenth century, the school had been languishing in its dirty downtown neighborhood. Despite heroic faculty and administrators, it needed more money, more students, and, most of all, a larger and more appealing campus.

In 1891, Brookings had joined the university's board at the urging of Samuel Cupples, a board member himself and Brookings's partner in an enormously profitable woodenware company, the largest of its kind in the country. As a young man, Brookings had moved to St. Louis from Maryland and begun working for the firm, becoming a successful and at times ruthless salesman. "I chased fortune and knifed my competitors," he later admitted. He and

Forest Park Terrace along Lindell, 1920. Robert Brookings's residence is at the far left.

Robert Brookings's caricature, with Washington University buildings and Cupples Station warehouse in the background

KNIFING COMPETITORS AND BUILDING WASHINGTON UNIVERSITY

Robert Brookings, the business-man who brought the School of Medicine to the Central West End, had little formal education himself. When he was a young boy, his father died, and he grew up on a farm near Baltimore, attending a crowded local school. At sixteen, he quit and came West, joining an older brother in a young business, Cupples & Marston, in St. Louis.

Rising through the ranks, he became a "fiddling drummer" or salesman, traveling some three hundred days a year all over the West. He was a smashing success, making the company and himself rich in the process. Then, like the firm's head Samuel Cupples, he sought a new purpose in life and embraced philanthropy, primarily at Washington University.

By 1909, he had won renown for his business acumen and good works. The Republican Party begged him to run for the US Senate, but he gave up that chance to take charge of re-establishing the medical school on its new Kingshighway campus. Still, during World War I, he had a chance to serve in government as a member of President Woodrow Wilson's Price Fixing Committee. Then in 1927, he founded the Brookings Institution, still a prominent Washington, D.C., think tank.

Robert Brookings's colonnaded home at 5125 Lindell

Cupples, his mentor and father figure, amassed a second fortune by building the Cupples Station complex, a string of warehouse depots in downtown St. Louis for trains unloading freight.

As Washington University board chairman in 1895, Brookings embarked on an in-depth study of the school and its needs, and four years later threw himself into the massive effort of relocating its undergraduate program. After exploring several parcels on horseback, he chose a splendid hilltop site on the western edge of Forest Park with a commanding view of the nascent Central West End. Because Brookings shrewdly leased the first group of buildings to the World's Fair for a sizeable profit, impatient students couldn't move in until 1905, but they were soon reveling in the luxurious space. "Here at long last," sighed student Alexander Langsdorf, "was the living realization of a dream come true." Next, Brookings, a dapper and highly eligible bachelor who didn't marry until he was seventy-seven years old, constructed more campus buildings with money he wheedled from older widows wishing to honor their late husbands.

**Samuel Cupples
(1831–1912)**

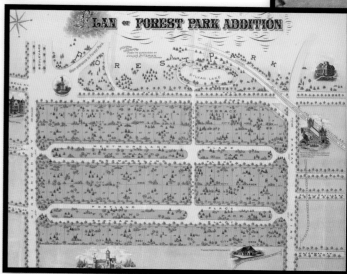

**Map of Forest Park Addition, designed
and constructed by Julius Pitzman**

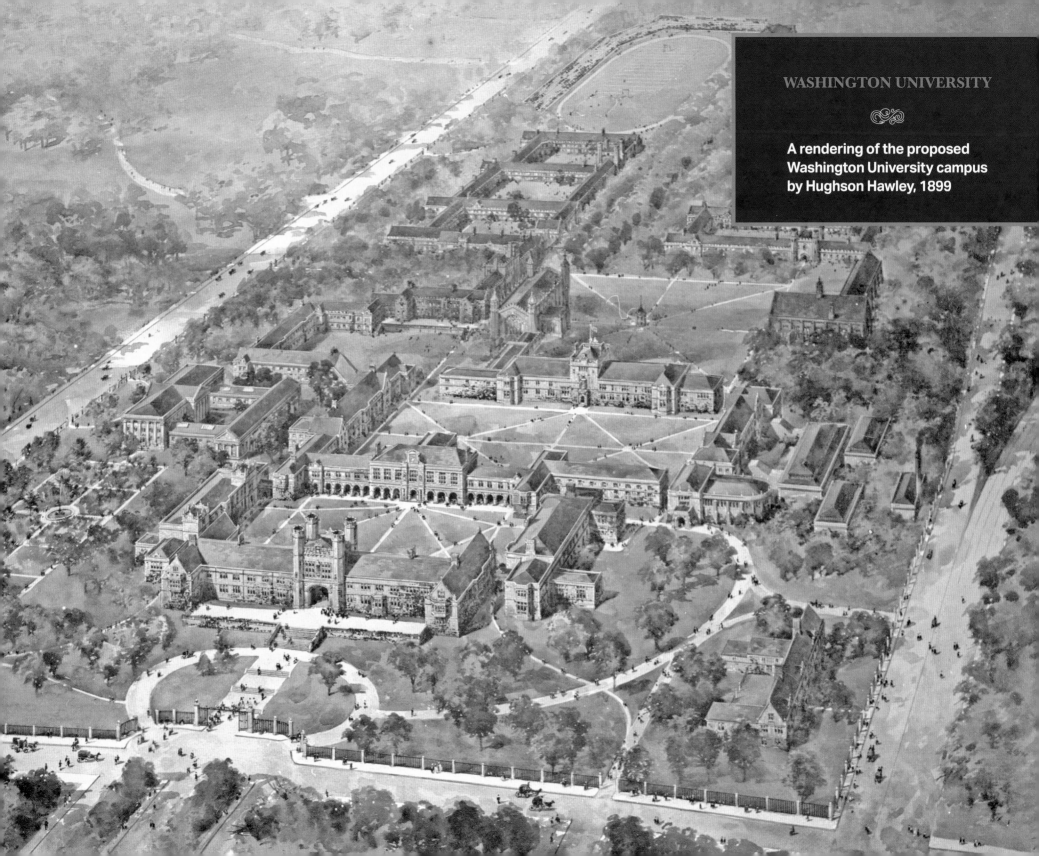

A rendering of the proposed Washington University campus by Hughson Hawley, 1899

Top left, exterior of Graham Chapel.
Right, construction of Brookings Hall.
Bottom left, campus construction, all early 1900s.

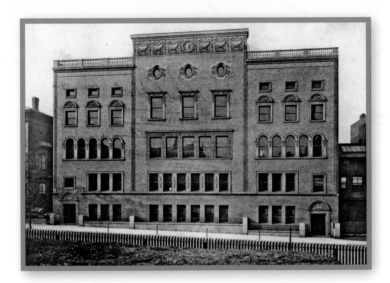

St. Louis Medical College, which in 1891 became the Medical Department of Washington University

Abraham Flexner
(1866–1959)

A SECOND "DREAM COME TRUE"

With the undergraduate campus well in hand, Brookings felt comfortable—even cocky—about the state of the university. In 1891, a medical department had formed through the acquisition of an existing school, the St. Louis Medical College, along with its archrival, the Missouri Medical College, eight years later. In 1905, Brookings and Adolphus Busch wiped out this new school's debt with handsome gifts of $25,000 each. But it had a poorly organized part-time faculty, deteriorating buildings, and a hospital in sad need of replacement. Said one of the medical students, "The floors are dirty; tables, chairs, everything covered with the grime and soot of years. This in a school where professors are trying to teach methods of strictest cleanliness."

Its deficiencies came to light in April 1909, when Abraham Flexner—an educator hired by the Carnegie Foundation for the Advancement of Teaching to do a nationwide survey of medical schools and assess their quality—came to St. Louis and looked over Washington University's medical program. As he wrote later, he found it "a little better than the worst I had seen elsewhere, but absolutely inadequate in every essential respect." At first, Brookings was indignant; after Flexner showed him the school's imperfections, he had to admit that it needed fundamental change. With the support of Chancellor David Houston, he formed a reorganization committee composed of his friends Robert McKittrick Jones, William K. Bixby, and Edward Mallinckrodt. Both Jones and Bixby were also his neighbors. Jones, a banker and dry goods merchant, lived with his wife, Grace Richards Jones, just behind Brookings at 6 Westmoreland Place, and the three often dined together.

Flexner returned to St. Louis and presented his findings to this committee, offering them some blunt advice: "Abolish the school. . . . Form a new faculty, reorganize your clinical facilities from top to bottom, and raise an endowment which will enable you to repeat in St. Louis what President Gilman [of Johns Hopkins] accomplished in Baltimore." It was a tall order, but the group bravely decided to proceed. On Flexner's advice, Brookings and Houston imported a faculty of stellar clinicians and researchers, largely from eastern schools, who were slyly known as the "Wise Men from the East." But to fully imitate Johns Hopkins, the new medical school would need to affiliate with a fine hospital—and Brookings knew which to target.

Through all these years, a new hospital for the city had been slowly but steadily inching toward existence. When the childless wholesale grocer and banker Robert Barnes died in 1891, he left his fortune to establish a facility "for sick and

"Certainly, a lot of the infrastructure in the Central West End helped bring Washington University's medical school here in the first place. Forest Park was a great amenity to have next to a hospital and medical school. The streetcar system was also important. When they dedicated the medical school buildings, Robert Brookings said that they were much farther out than they had been, but they were building such wonderful facilities that people would still want to come here, even though they were at the far western boundaries of the city."

—Philip Skroska,
Becker Library archivist

Robert Barnes (1808–1892)

Samuel Kennard (1842–1916)

injured persons, without distinction of creed, under the auspices of the Methodist Episcopal Church, South." He placed his bequest—$100,000 for the building and $850,000 for the endowment—in the hands of a few trusted executors, including Samuel Kennard of Portland Place. Later, Samuel Cupples joined the team, which tended and reinvested the fund brilliantly. Despite strident newspaper stories accusing them of tardiness, they waited patiently until they had enough money for the kind of hospital they had envisioned.

Once the capital had grown substantially—to $1.5 million by 1904—the trustees bought eight acres of land along Kingshighway and hired architect Theodore Link to design the new buildings. Fortuitously, Samuel Cupples was by then chairman of the Barnes executors. He and Brookings worked out a deal to affiliate and locate his medical school on adjacent property. Further, Brookings convinced his friend Grace Richards Jones, longtime head of the board of managers for St. Louis Children's Hospital, that her hospital, then in midtown St. Louis and in need of expansion, should move to the same campus.

Barnes Hospital construction, 1913–1914

First surgery, an appendectomy, performed at Barnes Hospital, 1914

Anatomy amphitheater, 1918

TWO YEARS, TWO HOSPITALS— THEN MORE

Within two years, three major building groups were dedicated on the Kingshighway campus. First came Barnes Hospital, which the *St. Louis Star* called "the largest and most efficiently equipped institution in the West," on October 28, 1914. In attendance were three thousand notable St. Louisans, among them David Francis, Isaac Lionberger, William Bixby, and Edward Mallinckrodt. The trustees of the Robert Barnes will, who by their prudent management had made this day possible, were also there, seated in the Barnes rotunda next to a bronze bust of Barnes. On December 7, 1914, the paper said, the hospital "formally opened with twenty-seven patients being cared for by 100 nurses and twenty-six resident doctors. . . . There are 373 more beds available and these are expected to be filled shortly."

Also on December 7, some tiny patients were transferred from the old Children's Hospital on Jefferson Avenue to its brand-new facility at 500 Kingshighway. This new campus represents "the last idea in modern hospital efficiency," boasted the *St. Louis Post-Dispatch*, and its two buildings "conform in architecture to the Barnes hospital nearby. . . .

St. Louis Children's Hospital
cornerstone laying, 1913

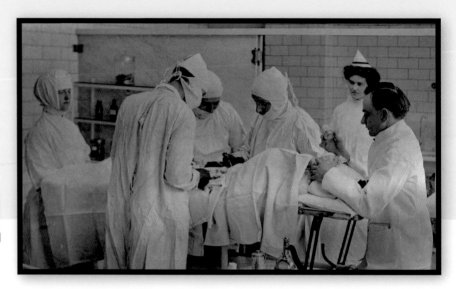

Children's Hospital
operating room, 1911

Every modern convenience for the children and the nurses has been installed. The babies' bathtubs are built high so that the nurse need not stoop. The faucets are operated by a pressure of the knee, and the nurses are summoned from one department to another by announcers such as are used at railway stations." The

official dedication of Children's Hospital came on January 9, 1915, with Grace Jones receiving keys to the building on behalf of the board. Physician Borden Veeder spoke, dedicating the work of the new hospital to its patients. "The one question we ask ourselves," he said, "is, 'How can we be of service to the community?'"

"When Barnes Hospital opened in 1914, it was a really big deal. This was easily the nicest hospital in the region, it was probably the nicest in the country, and from day one it was always one of the top hospitals in the world in terms of the facilities, the staff, the services offered, and the quality of care. So it really started off with a bang—and it has remained at the top for one hundred years."

—Stephen Logsdon,
Becker Library archivist

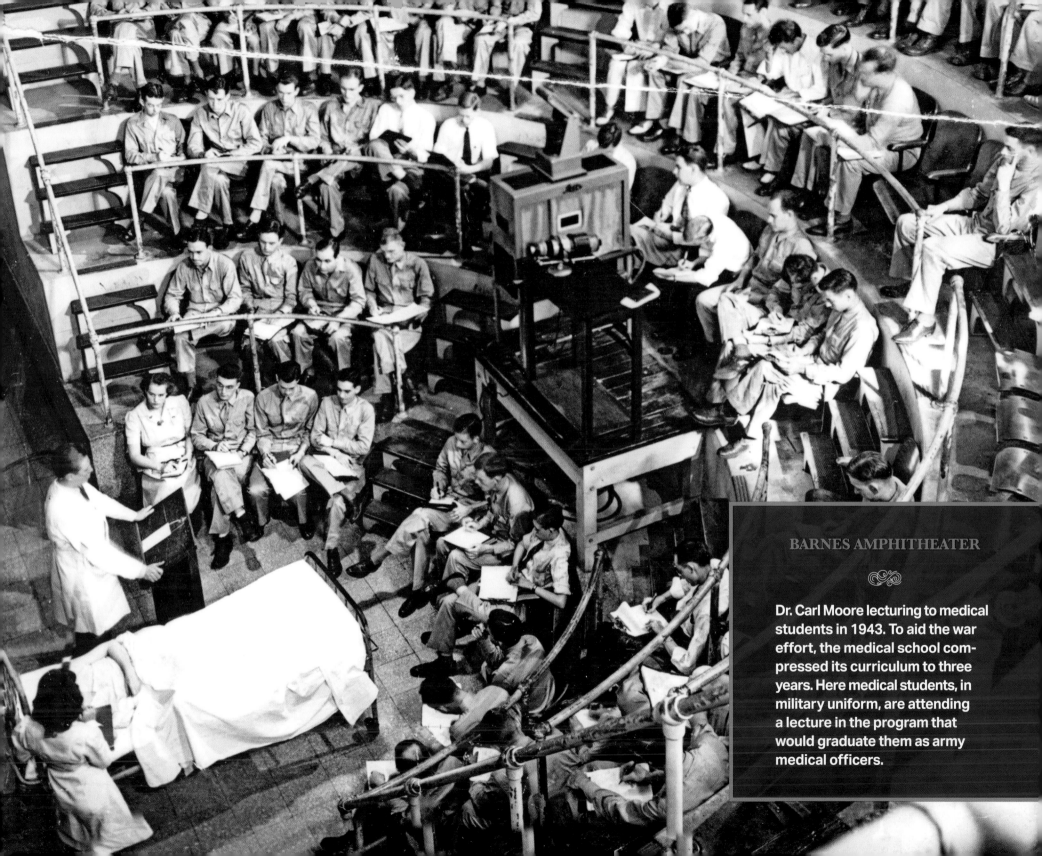

Top right, Washington University School of Medicine library, c. 1914. *Bottom right,* streetcar in front of Barnes West Building, 1926. *Bottom center,* Women's Surgical Ward, 1925. *Bottom left,* dispensary, c. 1914. *Top left,* dispensary corridor, c. 1914.

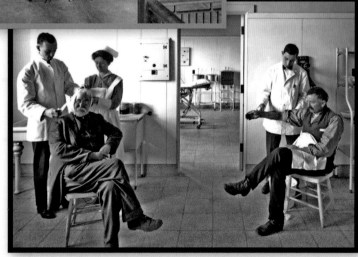

Cornerstone laying for the medical school's North Building; Robert Brookings on the right, May 17, 1913

The Barnes/Washington University School of Medicine complex, c. 1916

The capstone of all these events came on April 29, 1915. That morning, St. Louis newspapers were full of the news that the reorganized medical school—"an institution costing $1,200,000," reported the *St. Louis Star* breathlessly—was being dedicated in a three-day ceremony attended by university presidents and even a few visitors from abroad, who managed to make the trip despite the war raging in Europe. Robert Brookings was the hero of the day with papers trumpeting his $1 million gift that had made this new school possible. As Acting Chancellor Frederic A. Hall said, Brookings was "the one man, pre-eminently, whose dream is this day realized."

The new school's Central West End neighborhood was quickly becoming a haven for hospitals. In May 1904, St. Luke's Hospital had dedicated a large hospital and nurses' home on Delmar and Belt, moving from its previous location at Nineteenth and Washington. St. John's Mercy, founded in 1871 by the Sisters of Mercy as an affiliate of the Missouri Medical College, had moved to 307 North Euclid in 1912 from a previous location at Twenty-Third and Locust. The Missouri Baptist Sanitarium (later Hospital) was built in 1897 as a free dispensary for the poor at 909 North Taylor.

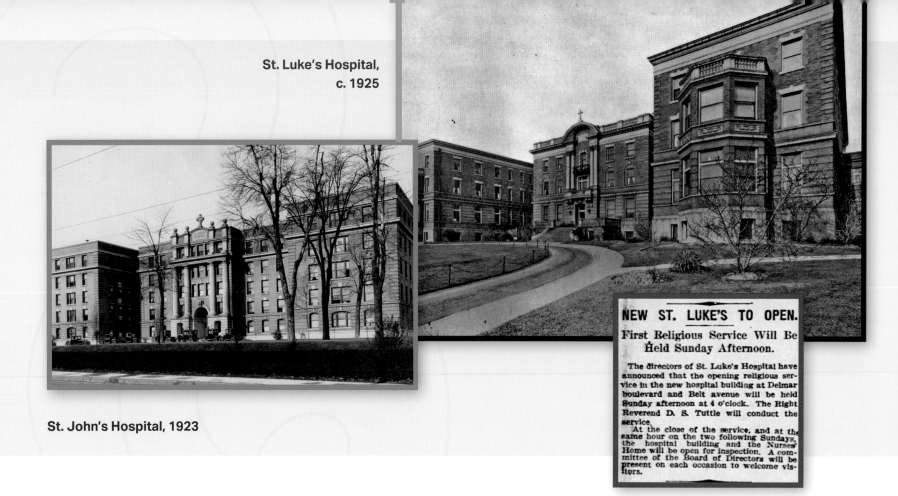

St. Luke's Hospital, c. 1925

St. John's Hospital, 1923

NEW ST. LUKE'S TO OPEN.

First Religious Service Will Be Held Sunday Afternoon.

The directors of St. Luke's Hospital have announced that the opening religious service in the new hospital building at Delmar boulevard and Belt avenue will be held Sunday afternoon at 4 o'clock. The Right Reverend D. S. Tuttle will conduct the service.

At the close of the service, and at the same hour on the two following Sundays, the hospital building and the Nurses' Home will be open for inspection. A committee of the Board of Directors will be present on each occasion to welcome visitors.

And there were more to come. One was the 130-bed Liberty Hospital, built at Taylor and Washington in 1922, which was sold in 1930; another was the Shriner's Hospital, which located at Euclid and Clayton in 1924. Two years later, not long before the Depression quashed further plans for expansion, Jewish Hospital left its original site on Delmar for a fine seven-story, 250-bed home at 216 Kingshighway, just north of the Barnes Hospital and School of Medicine complex.

The move had a hefty $2.5 million price tag, but the planners wanted to create "what stands as the last word in hospital development in this country," said a 1926 story. This building had everything they hoped for, from the latest technology to elegant aesthetics: a marble-wainscoted lobby, halls with terrazzo floors, rooms with up-to-date technology, and a roof garden with "a splendid view" of Forest Park.

Top, Jewish Hospital dedication, 1902. *Middle,* Jewish Hospital patients. *Bottom right,* Jewish Hospital postcard, 1918. *Bottom center,* Shriner's Hospital. *Bottom left,* Liberty Hospital, Taylor and Washington, 1923.

A FLOURISHING BUSINESS DISTRICT

Along with strong medical care, the affluent Central West End population stimulated the rise of other supporting institutions, such as shops, churches, and social venues. In 1912, newspapers reported rapid growth on Olive at Taylor with the successful Beethoven and Lister office buildings completed and another going up on the remaining corner. At 4451 and 4453 Olive, a new headquarters was planned for Wright and Gilmore interior decorators. Nearby, a six-story "bachelor apartment building"—which "will include a swimming pool and other novel features," said the *Post-Dispatch*—was on the drawing board.

The swarm of new businesses in the area included the Luyties Homeopathic Pharmacy Company at 4200 Laclede Avenue. Its unusual, poured-concrete building, one of the earliest examples of this construction style in St. Louis, was designed by architect Frederick Bonsack in 1915 for the thriving company, whose earlier Central West End building was destroyed in a fire. At the time, homeopathic medicine—based on the theory that diseases can often be cured by giving the patient tiny doses of a substance that would, in larger doses, create symptoms like the ones that need curing—was popular. The founder of this company, Herman C. G. Luyties, had opened the first homeopathic pharmacy in

GREAT ACTIVITY IN TWO TRACTS IN THE WEST END

Investors Are Eagerly Buying Choice Lots and Building Operations Indicate That They Will Be Rivals of City's Choicest Residence Districts.

St. Louis Post-Dispatch, **April 7, 1912**

Road work on Sarah and Washington, c. 1915

Bissinger's, *St. Louis Post-Dispatch,* **March 3, 1946**

St. Louis in 1853 to serve the city's many practitioners, and it grew into a business with a worldwide clientele.

In 1927, Karl Bissinger left his family chocolate business near Cincinnati, Ohio, to come to St. Louis and start his own confectionery, which he opened in a wood-paneled space at 4742 McPherson Avenue that was reminiscent of European shops. An ad from 1927 touted "French Confections, Special Candies Made to Order," later adding, at the height of the Depression, "We Deliver Free." After Bissinger's death in 1946, his employees took over the business, but in 1974 they sold it to new owners. The long-time McPherson location closed in 2007, and Bissinger's moved a few blocks away to Maryland Plaza.

J. Arthur Anderson Laundry, headquartered at 3970 Olive Street, was "one of the most interesting places in St. Louis for visiting laundrymen," said the *Post-Dispatch,* because of its "new and original ideas." By 1910, it had opened an annex on McPherson near Euclid, where it demonstrated "how high-class family washing should be done." But the laundry contended that it could not comply with the anti-smoke ordinance. In 1917, it offered $50 to the pro-abatement Civic League if it could find anyone to run its furnaces for two months without violating the ordinance. Then in 1927, it opened a new facility at 4940 Washington

Below, road work at Sarah and Washington, c. 1915. *Facing page, top,* Pierce-Arrow showroom, 4733 McPherson. *Facing page, bottom right,* Sarah-Olive Bank, 1931. *Facing page, middle,* Congress Theater, 4000 Olive, 1928. *Facing page, bottom left,* West End Lyric Theater, 4819 Delmar, 1937.

Avenue, a Beaux-Arts building with a semicircular driveway and turtles crawling across its facade, with an inscription: "Slow and Careful."

By 1935, the Central West End was home to stylish shops that catered to the wealthy: Carson Linen Shop at 232 North Euclid ("Linens, Sport Robes for all Occasions"); Carton's, 4914 Maryland ("Gifts of China, Glassware and Silver"); Rosenheim Shop, 4409 West Pine ("Smart Clothes for Women and Débutantes"); R. E. Starkey Shop, 4510 Maryland ("Individually Designed Millinery"); Madeleine Et Cie, Park Plaza ("Gowns"); Ernst Oertel Inc., 4914 Maryland ("Quality Furrier"); Charlotte Wagner Corset Shop, 236 North Euclid; Georgian House, 4942 Maryland ("Old English Silver and Sheffield Plate"); Joseph Witek Florist, 4732 McPherson; and Pierce-Arrow St. Louis Inc., 4733 McPherson ("Pierce-Arrow Service in St. Louis for 20 Years.")

The Woman's Exchange, founded in 1883, had also followed the westward progress of the well-to-do, moving from North Sixth Street in downtown St. Louis to Locust, Olive, and North Grand Avenue. Then came two locations on Euclid, where they advertized "Children's Dresses and Toys, Tea Room, Bakery Dept., Gifts," adding "we are the only organized institution incorporated for charitable purposes. . . ." Finally, they settled at 1 Maryland Plaza, where they sold items and their trademark sandwiches to such celebrities as the wife of Arnold Palmer, the wives of the football Cardinals, and Liberace.

Occasionally, they partnered with the Junior League, founded in 1914, whose members often lived in the Central West End. In 1933, the Woman's Exchange staged a fashion show for children at the Junior League lunchroom, 4914 Maryland, in which sons and daughters of League members modeled "sun suits for back yards and beaches, party frocks and accessories, and street and play outfits" while showcasing toys made by occupational therapy patients.

EDUCATIONAL LIFE BLOSSOMS

To serve the burgeoning Central West End population, schools of all kinds sprang up: private and public, religious and secular, single-sex and coed. The best-known private schools were Smith Academy and Mary Institute, founded as secondary divisions of Washington University. For many years, Smith Academy—attended by some of the city's most socially prominent young men, including poet T. S. Eliot— remained at its increasingly unfashionable site in downtown St. Louis. In 1905, the school moved to a new building on Enright Avenue off Union just north of the Central West

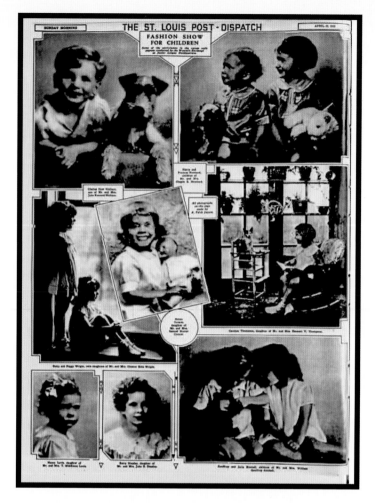

Junior League Fashion Show for Children, 1933

Mary Institute facade, Lake Avenue, undated

Class of 1924 in front of Mary Institute, Lake Avenue

End, where it adjoined another of the university's secondary divisions, the Manual Training School. In 1917, the entire campus was sold to the Board of Education.

In 1902, Mary Institute was still at its second location on Locust and Beaumont, "in the midst of a teeming city, rather than in a desirable suburban location . . .," said a Mary Institute history. "[S]omething had to be done." Just then, benefactors William and Eliza McMillan, whose fortune came from the Missouri Car & Foundry Company, donated $100,000 toward a brand-new brick building at Lake and Waterman. At the groundbreaking ceremony in 1901, physician Abigail Eliot—granddaughter of William Greenleaf Eliot, whose late daughter Mary had provided the school's name—turned over the first shovelful of dirt. During its years in the Central West End, the school added a new assembly hall, British poet John Masefield came to speak in 1916, and the girls held "Patriotic Lunches" during World War I. All the while, its enrollment continued to burgeon, and it needed more outdoor space. In 1930, it moved to its "country home" in Ladue.

Adjacent to the grand home of David Francis on Maryland, the Sisters of the Sacred Heart bought a large piece of property and built a red brick and stone school building with a marble statue of Sacré Coeur out front. Inside was a chapel that had an altar and pedestals created by Louis Comfort Tiffany. In 1883, this City House of the Academy of the Sacred Heart opened to 115 girls, but soon parents were lobbying for a companion boys' school—so the nuns founded Barat Hall and added a new classroom wing in 1913 to accommodate it.

News stories in 1900 announced that contracts were being let for the Eugene Field School, named for the St. Louis journalist and children's poet, at Olive and Taylor. "The building is constructed in the double wing style, with entrances for boys and girls respectively in the right and left wing fronts on Olive Street," said one 1900 story. "The center of the structure sets back, forming an open court in front of which a tall flagstaff will float the American flag." The school opened in 1901 with seven hundred students. A story that year in the *St. Louis Republic* noted that, before and after school, students were flocking to Carrie Whitcomb's confectionery at 4052 Olive—"[and] a busy scene is enacted as the little ones clamber around her, holding up their pennies, nickels and dimes, some wanting candy, some sandwiches, others fruit and even pickles."

Another school, opened in 1925 at 4568 Forest Park Avenue, was the Elias Michael School for Crippled

Patricia Hannagan crowning a statue of the Blessed Virgin at the City House of Sacred Heart Academy, Maryland and Taylor avenues, *St. Louis Star-Times*, June 1, 1938

Eugene Field School, Olive Street and Taylor, 1900

Above, **students at Elias Michael School, 1940.** *Left,* **Rachel Stix Michael at a testimonial luncheon, 1934.**

Moving the Joseph Hayes residence, 4389 Lindell, to make way for the Rosati-Kain Catholic High School for Girls, 1921

Children. Its name honored Elias Michael, a school board member and president of the Rice-Stix Dry Goods Company, whose widow—Rachel Stix Michael—had herself been appointed to the board by Mayor Henry Kiel in 1922. She was a tireless volunteer whose special cause was the welfare of children; her only child, Selma, had died at age seven in 1894. She urged the city to establish a school for handicapped children and even brought in consultants at her own expense. After the Elias Michael School opened, she pushed the city to open a school for handicapped African American children, the Turner School for Negro Cripples. She won the governor's medallion for distinguished public service in 1933.

In 1915, Archbishop John J. Glennon announced that a new Cathedral School to accommodate some four hundred children would be built on one of two sites near the New Cathedral. "This will be the first time the Cathedral of St. Louis ever has had its own school," said an announcement. And Rosati-Kain Catholic High School for Girls, formerly at Grand and Lucas Avenues, moved to Newstead and Lindell in 1921 at a cost of $225,000. To make way for its construction, a house formerly owned by Joseph Hayes had to be moved off the site.

Delmar Baptist Church, 1902

Rev. George Dodson, 1903

A THRIVING RELIGIOUS COMMUNITY

Along with the congregations that had located in the Central West End in earlier decades, others were established there or moved to the neighborhood during this period. In 1914, one stalwart West End church was just changing hands. Delmar Baptist, then on the corner of Delmar and Pendleton, was moving west to a new building at Skinker and Washington designed by noted school architect William B. Ittner. The old building went first to the First Church of the Nazarene and then, in 1947, to its current congregation, Galilee Baptist Church. Then in 1917, the Church of the Unity was designed by William B. Ittner and built at 5007 Waterman in the early Gothic style. The church, previously at Park and Armstrong Avenues, merged with First Unitarian Church and took that name. One longtime pastor was George Dodson, who came in 1903 with a PhD from Harvard and remained for decades. In a newspaper account, he explained the 1917 move by saying that "his parish is metropolitan, drawing largely from the West End and suburbs."

In 1917, Albert Groves, who had designed the nearby Tuscan Masonic Temple, was also the architect of the English Gothic–style Westminster Presbyterian Church at Delmar and Union, built at a cost of $175,000. In 1917, the *Star*

Westminster Presbyterian Church, 5318 Delmar, built in 1916, was designed by Albert Groves in 1935

Holy Corners, 1920s

reported on a controversy involving Westminster, "one of the most exclusive churches in the city." With World War I under way in Europe, its pastor, Rev. John F. Cannon, opposed the singing of patriotic songs in church unless they were also "worshipful," since "he does not allow patriotism to take the place of religion." North of Delmar were two other churches attended by Central West End residents: Pilgrim Congregational, which moved to this site from Washington and Ewing in 1906; and Union Avenue Christian Church, also designed by Albert Groves, with its elegant sanctuary completed in 1908.

At the corner of Lindell and Newstead across from the New Cathedral was the Lindell Avenue Methodist Episcopal Church, where the John Kauffman family worshiped. In 1896, the church had built a chapel and four years later the sanctuary, but in 1913 they changed their minds and decided to move a bit farther west to 340 North Skinker at Waterman. Instead of selling their old building, they had it dismantled, stone by stone, and resurrected on Skinker, where the church—

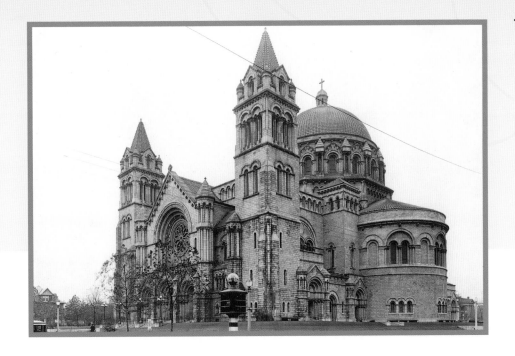

The New Cathedral, 1929

The design for St. Nicholas Greek Orthodox Church, Forest Park Avenue, 1930

now Grace Methodist—was rededicated in October 1914. Among its fittings is a marble baptismal font decorated with intertwined flowers honoring Kauffman's daughters, Violet and Marguerite. In December 1930, the membership of St. Nicholas Greek Orthodox Church broke ground for a sanctuary to occupy its new site on Forest Park Avenue and Kingshighway. The church, which had lost its previous building on Garrison and St. Louis in the 1927 tornado, had rented an empty synagogue at Kingshighway and Enright, and then

spent some $250,000 to build this new space for its 5,000-member congregation. Some of those members, wrote Mary Stiritz in her book, *St Louis: Historic Churches & Synagogues*, lived in the area. "By 1916, St. Louis' growing Greek settlement . . . owned more than 400 small businesses, including several movie houses and a large number of West End restaurants."

Yet another historic church left the area in 1930. St. George's Episcopal Church on Pendleton at Olive had built this structure in 1891 after its previous church at Chestnut and Beaumont went up in flames. But financial problems plagued the congregation, and a note in an 1895 *Post-Dispatch* article explained one reason why: "It is generally admitted that Rev. R.A. Holland of St. George's is the best-paid of local Episcopal clergymen, and he declared in the course of debate at the last diocesan convention that he gets $5,000 a year." So money woes forced the congregation—"one of the oldest in the city," said a *Post-Dispatch* article—to make a decision in 1928: move or merge? They rejected an alliance with another Central West End congregation, the Church of the Redeemer at Euclid and Washington, but decided to merge with St. Michael and All Angels Church, forming the current St. Michael and St. George on Wydown Boulevard. They sold their Pendleton church to St. Stephen's Lutheran for $29,500.

Then in 1935, Trinity Episcopal Church moved west from 4005 Washington to a building at Euclid and Washington, empty since the closing of another congregation, the Church of the Redeemer. Originally, this building was the sanctuary of St. James' Church, which had moved it, stone by stone, from its original location. In November 1935, historic Trinity Church, founded in 1855, celebrated its rededication and added to the chancel a medieval-style crucifix designed by

The Episcopal Church of the Redeemer, Washington and Euclid, 1910

Trinity Episcopal, undated. *Inset,* Rev. George Betts, who became pastor in 1876.

ST. GEORGE'S CHURCH

St. George's Church, later
St. Stephen's Lutheran
Church, Pendleton and Olive

Temple Israel, Washington at Kingshighway, undated

Eames and Walsh and sculpted by Victor Berlindis, a member of the parish.

In addition to Temple Israel, other Jewish synagogues clustered in and around the Central West End. B'rith Sholom Congregation, established in 1908, settled in a small synagogue at 6166 Delmar. Down the street at Delmar and Clara was another congregation, B'nai El, which had moved from Spring and Flad to occupy the former Central Presbyterian Church building in 1930. A *Post-Dispatch* article about clerical salaries mentioned that the rabbi of B'nai El was the third highest paid in the area at $2,400 a year. Still, that was far below the salary of Rev. Leon Harrison, rabbi of Temple Israel, who—like the highest-paid Protestant ministers in the area—earned $6,000 a year. Members of these Jewish congregations used the funeral services of Berger Memorial Chapel, founded by Hungarian immigrant Henry Berger in 1896 and established in 1916 on McPherson in the Central West End, where it remained until 2013.

CAMPAIGN AGAINST IMPROPER DANCING

Teachers to Send Lecturers Before Municipal Community Centers Here.

The Protective Association of Teachers of Dancing of St. Louis, at a meeting yesterday at the academy of Jacob Mahler, 4911 Washington boulevard, agreed to send members to lecture at each of the municipal community centers on the subject of proper dancing, postures, steps and movements.

This action was taken in response to a request from Director of Public Playgrounds Abeken and is a part of an extensive program of publicity by the association in the interests of cleaner dancing. A communication from the Catholic Knights of America requesting that a speaker be appointed to address that organization at an early date was favorably acted upon.

Because the pending dance hall ordinance, which the Board of Aldermen ordered engrossed last week, contains no provisions for dance hall inspectors, but assigns the work of regulation and inspection to specially appointed members of the Police Department, it was decided to supply the Police Department, the dance halls and the general public with posed photographs of correct dancing positions.

C. A. Neville, secretary of the association, denounced the animal

---

INSTRUCTORS PLAN CAMPAIGN AGAINST IMPROPER DANCING

"The Protective Association of Teachers of Dancing of St. Louis, at a meeting yesterday at the academy of Jacob Mahler, 4911 Washington boulevard, agreed to send members to lecture at each of the municipal community centers on the subject of proper dancing, postures, steps, and movements.

"This action was taken . . . [as] part of an extensive program of publicity by the association in the interests of cleaner dancing. . . . Because the pending dance hall ordinance, which the board of aldermen ordered . . . last week, contains no provisions for dance hall inspectors, but assigns the work of regulation and inspection to specially appointed members of the Police Department, it was decided to supply the Police Department, the dance halls and the general public with posed photographs of correct dancing positions.

"C. A. Neville, secretary of the association, denounced the animal dances, fox trot, shimmy, kitchen sink, camel walk, angleworm wiggle and others. He proposed that the association go on record against them.

"The motion was carried."

"LEADERS OF SOCIAL LIFE"

But these Central West End residents also had fun. After Albert Mahler immigrated to St. Louis from France, he opened a downtown dance academy, which his son Jacob took over in 1875. In 1907, with his customer base moving west, Jacob commissioned Theodore Link to design a building at 4915 Washington as his home and ballroom. Until his death in 1928, Jacob reigned there as "an instructor of future leaders of social life, an arbiter of refinement, and a master of ceremonies," said a *Post-Dispatch* obituary. In his role as impresario, he "occupied the limelight" at many Veiled Prophet balls, where "thirty-six of the women who were chosen as queens of the prophet's court had been his dancing pupils." On Friday evenings, he held "Fortnightlies": dances for teenagers from prominent families.

Lindell Boulevard was the site of several social organizations that catered to well-to-do members. Close to the eastern boundary of the area but easily accessible to Central West End residents was the giant, lavishly decorated Columbian Club, designed by Alfred Rosenheim in the Italian Renaissance style and built by the Columbians, an exclusive Jewish organization. "It Is by Far the Handsomest and Most Gorgeous Club-House in St. Louis—A Ballroom

Columbian Club, 3917 Lindell, designed by Alfred Rosenheim, 1924

Drawings of the stairway and one of the large fireplaces, Columbian Club, *St. Louis Post-Dispatch* June 24, 1894

PORTRAIT OF A LINDELL SITE:
THE ENGINEERS' CLUB OF ST. LOUIS

In 1868, a group of local professionals—including James Eads, civil engineer, builder of ironclad gunboats during the Civil War, and designer of the Eads Bridge—founded the the Engineers' Club of St. Louis. Early on, the club held its meetings on the first Washington University campus downtown or at the Elks Club. Then they rented clubrooms on Lucas and on Pine, before moving to the Academy of Science building at 3817 Olive.

The growing organization wanted its own space, and in 1914 they established a building fund to make that possible. Progress was slow, but in 1924 they finally bought the vacant Nugent mansion at 4359 Lindell and spent the next two years fixing it up, with labor donated by the members. At its dedication in 1926, the building had the same exterior but a 300-seat auditorium inside where four bedrooms had once been located.

Years went by, and the club was still getting larger, so it looked around for new locations. In 1946, they tried to buy a site at Wydown and Skinker but neighbors objected; in 1947, they tried and failed to buy a site on the southeast corner of Lindell and Kingshighway.

So in 1957, they made a new decision: tear down the Nugent building and build a new, more contemporary headquarters at their old Lindell location. By then, two neighboring lots were also vacant, so they bought those and incorporated them in the plan. Two years later, the club dedicated its $400,000, one-story building with a 400-seat auditorium. Today, it remains the headquarters for the club, which has more than one thousand members.

Archbishop Peter Kenrick (1806–1896)

Finished in Pure White—Some Pretty Corners," gushed the *Post-Dispatch* at the time of its opening. "Two thousand invitations have been sent out and all the elite of Jewish society are expected to be in attendance." In 1928, the building was sold to the Knights of Columbus, and six years later they resold it to the Automobile Club of Missouri, but it was destroyed in a 1935 fire.

Down the street was the St. Louis Woman's Club, established in 1903 "to provide hospitality to the wives of the heads of state and royalty visiting St. Louis during the 1904 World's Fair," said a club history. In 1912, it moved from rented quarters at 3621 Washington Boulevard to 4600 Lindell, formerly the William Donaldson home, which it purchased for $40,000. Neighbors "objected vigorously when they learned that a club was to invade their exclusive residence neighborhood," said the *Post-Dispatch*, but opposition seems to have melted away, and the club soon added a ballroom and café. "The functions of the St. Louis Woman's Club are always ultra-fashionable and exclusive," added a 1912 *Star* story.

Also on Lindell were the two successive mansions of the Irish-born Catholic prelate, John J. Glennon, who was installed as St. Louis's fourth archbishop in 1903 and named a cardinal shortly before his death in 1946. First he lived in

WOMAN'S CLUB IS NOT WELCOME AT NO. 4600 LINDELL

Organization Votes to Buy Donaldson Place, Despite Neighbors' Protests.

ANSWERS   OBJECTIONS

Members Say Organization Doesn't Draw Delivery Wagons —No Bar in Place.

The St. Louis Woman's Club, most exclusive of society organizations, has been surprised to learn in the last few days that some wealthy owners of homes near its proposed new location, at 4600 Lindell boulevard, do not want the club as a neighbor.

The club voted Monday to buy William R. Donaldson's residence, at the number named, for $40,000. This action was taken after the reading and discussion of protests which neighbors of the Donaldsons have sent to them and to the club against the transaction.

Mrs. A. D. Brown, wife of a millionaire shoe manufacturer, who lives the next door west of the Donaldson house, is said to be one of the objectors. Some of the residents of adjoining houses are

St. Louis Post-Dispatch, **December 11, 1911**

Top, the Winter Garden ice skating rink in the Jai Alai Building at DeBaliviere and Kingsbury, c. 1960. *Bottom,* interior of the Winter Garden.

the grand, Romanesque-style residence built for Archbishop Peter Kenrick at 3810 Lindell in 1891. In 1923, Archbishop Glennon moved west to an elegant 11,000-square-foot home at 4510 Lindell, built by banker and brewer William Nolker in 1891. In a 1902 *National Magazine* article, one writer called the house "A Rhine Inspiration on Lindell Boulevard."

Near the western edge of the Central West End was the Winter Garden skating rink at 520 DeBaliviere. It began life during the World's Fair as a venue for the sport of jai alai; then the "Jai Alai Building" became a roller skating rink; and in 1916, the owners announced that it would be renovated as an indoor ice-skating rink that could accommodate two thousand skaters and one thousand spectators. At its grand opening that November, "St. Louis will have its first peep at the continental skate dances," raved a *Star* news story, adding that a famous skating couple would appear to present them. On the big day, the ice machines malfunctioned and a disappointed crowd had to content itself with "the privilege of inspecting the handsomely outfitted place," said another article.

Further down the street were other popular venues: the Dorr and Zeller Cafeteria; Garavelli's Restaurant, which had a posh décor including a crystal chandelier with a popular fountain underneath; Moll's, which advertised itself as

"St. Louis' Most Complete Food Market" and had an ornate clock out front. "DeBaliviere Avenue between 1920 and 1950 was a street of considerable commercial importance with major chain drug and food stores, the Apollo Theater, a Parkmoor, and Steve the Watermelon man's place at Pershing Avenue, which was a popular rendezvous for streetcar men," wrote Norbury Wayman. Movie theaters also served the area, including the Delmonte, which offered silent films on Delmar east of DeBaliviere, as well as the Pageant at Delmar and Laurel, which "had a 'skydome' open air theater . . . during the silent picture period."

Exterior of Garavelli's, 1932

Moll Grocery Company, Delmar and DeBaliviere, 1932

GARAVELLI'S RESTAURANT

Garavelli's dining room, 1930

Left, Chase and Park Plaza hotels as seen from Kingshighway, 1930. Top right, Chase Park Plaza entrance, c. 1925. Bottom right, night view of the Chase Park Plaza Hotel, c. 1940.

"THE CHASE IS THE PLACE"

During the 1910s and 1920s, a young Jewish couple with their own growing family—Sam and Jeannette Koplar— established a successful construction business that focused largely on Central West End properties. They built flats on Pershing and one of the first high-rise apartment buildings in St. Louis, the eight-story Westmoreland at 5360 Pershing, which they sold in 1918 for a substantial $400,000. In the early 1920s, the family embarked on a three-month trip to Europe to celebrate their success—and when they got back, they took on even bigger projects: building the Embassy Apartments at Union and Washington in 1926 and the Congress Hotel and Senate Apartments on Union in 1927.

But Sam was beguiled by the lavish Savoy Plaza Hotel in New York City, where his family had stayed on their way to Europe. In 1929, he began work on a St. Louis version to be located on the site of the old Kauffman/Bixby estate near Lindell and Kingshighway. Its close neighbor to the south would be the Chase Hotel (called "the miracle of the miracle city"): a nine-story, 500-bed hotel designed by architect Preston Bradshaw and built in 1922 by Chase Ulman. The "Park Plaza," as the new building would be called—"Plaza" for the Savoy Plaza and "Park" for Forest Park—would be designed in the Art Deco style and inside would feature

INCOHERENT BUT FABULOUS: THE KAUFFMAN/BIXBY MANSION

Before the Chase Park Plaza was a gleam in Sam Koplar's eye, that prime eight-acre site at Lindell and Kingshighway was occupied by a giant mansion built in 1885 by flour milling baron John W. Kauffman. Its style—a cheerful assortment of turrets, chimneys, and dormers—may have been "picturesque," admitted architectural critic Charges Savage, but it "was clumsy, lacking in any coherent unity."

The 45-room mansion and outbuildings, which cost some $200,000 to build, sprawled over a whole city block. Inside, the house was ornately furnished, sparing no expense. There were barrel-vaulted rooms, exquisitely decorated arches, and the city's largest private greenhouse.

After Kauffman's death in 1904, his widow, Nellie Bronson Kauffman, and their son Harold both moved to new houses on Portland Place. William Bixby bought part of the property (soon known as the "Bixby Farm") in 1902 and the rest in 1904. He and his large family lived there until 1920, and after their departure, the house was razed.

The Kauffman mansion, on the site of the present-day Chase Park Plaza, was later owned by William Bixby and then razed, 1921.

Vignette

The Park Plaza (*left***) and Chase Hotel (***right***) as seen from Forest Park, c. 1930**

big-city luxuries: velvet draperies, divans in the lobby, and uniformed bellhops. Newspapers reported that the project would cost $6 million, as "the tallest and most pretentious apartment [building] ever built in St. Louis."

But the Park Plaza was only partly finished on Tuesday, October 29, 1929—"Black Friday," the day that Wall Street crashed. When Sam Koplar's $4 million loan was suddenly withdrawn, he arranged for another and managed to complete his hotel, while personally supervising every inch of the construction. "I would walk through the rooms at night with a torch and examine the plastering. If I found rough places in closet corners, I would hack at them with a hatchet so they would be done over," he told the *Post-Dispatch* later. Another construction story became a kind of urban legend. He and a staff member were making rounds when they saw a worker, fast asleep. Sam's companion said, "Mr. Sam, I'll wake him up." "No, no, no," replied Sam. "Don't do that. As long as he's sleeping, he still has a job." The hotel opened, and Koplar struggled to keep it going, but the Park Plaza was taken over by its mortgage holder in 1937. The Chase Hotel had also fallen into foreclosure in 1931.

Still Sam Koplar didn't give up. He took a job as manager of the nearby Forest Park Hotel; Jeannette managed the Branscome Apartment Hotel, 5370 Pershing, which the family had bought in 1926; and they lived frugally. As Chase Hotel stock became available, Sam quietly began buying it up, while monitoring the changing ownership of the Park Plaza. As he said in 1958, the Park Plaza would always be "my baby, and I still think it's the most flexible hotel in the world."

FINE APARTMENTS GO UP

Sam Koplar was not the only builder interested in the Central West End. In 1908, a building permit was issued to the St. Regis Realty Co., with Claude Vrooman as president, to construct an eight-story building with 440 rooms called the St. Regis Apartments. "Grand Entrance to Forest Park," announced one *Star* ad, "magnificent in all its appointments and unsurpassed in everything constituting class and comfort." An article also predicted the development of Kingshighway, which "will be claimed . . . within a comparatively short time . . . by apartment houses and hotels. Advantageous apartment building sites . . . are yielding from $800 to $1500 a front foot."

"New $500,000 Building Seems Destined to Prove Highly Popular" said a 1910 headline about the Oxford, "the new, big, high-class apartment building at Union and McPherson Avenue, which is now ready for occupancy. . . . apartments already have been leased from the plans to a

The Chase Hotel with old cars out front, c. 1925

Advertising on Lindell, *St. Louis Post-Dispatch*, 1909

GOAT OR OLD GOAT?

In her book *St. Louis Lost*, author Mary Bartley tells the story of the thirty-room Houser mansion at 4545 West Pine Boulevard, built in 1893 with eleven fireplaces, a living room lined with Italian oak, and one mantelpiece topped with carved cupids. In 1916, the owners sold the house to Alan Baker, who brought four generations of his family to live there along with a host of animals. They stabled their horses—plus a sly, restless, yellow-bearded goat named Tony—in their elegant carriage house with mahogany stalls.

"Tony was not the ideal city pet, and one day he escaped," wrote Bartley. "[T]he police insisted on having a complete description—including height, weight, sex, and coloring of the missing beast.

"In a surprisingly short time, the authorities called with the happy news that they had located Tony. He had climbed the fire escape of the Kings-way/Ambassador Hotel, then located at Kingshighway and West Pine, and was found after an extremely agitated woman reported that 'an ugly old man with a filthy beard' was leering at her through the bedroom window."

ROOMS from $40 monthly

HOTEL KINGSWAY

Do as the smart St. Louisans do! Miss nothing of the gay life of St. Louis, yet dwell in home-like comfort . . . at the Kings-Way. Low tariffs for unusually fine rooms . . . not the least of many attractions you will find.

You will enjoy our sumptuous dining-room. Dinners from $1

Opposite Forest Park   *Under Schimmel Direction*

HOTEL KINGS-WAY

KINGSHIGHWAY *at* W. PINE

most desirable class of tenants." Not only was the building luxurious, went on the article, but "the location is high and healthful, and the building overlooks one of the most attractive thoroughfares in the city." In 1913, the *Post-Dispatch* reported that one of the residents of the Oxford Apartments was J. D. Wooster Lambert, who "has the largest income of any young man in St. Louis."

Then in 1925, a syndicate headed by A. D. Gates announced that it would be building a fourteen-story apartment building known as Hampden Hall at the southwest corner of Newstead and McPherson. Altogether, it would have fifty-two five- and six-room apartments. On the opposite corner would be the new Greystone; like its companion, it would have a basement garage for fifty-two cars. These were fine addresses, suitable for a bit of boasting. One 1927 society note announced that, "James Hamilton Grover of the Hotel Chase has taken an apartment in the Greystone. . . . His daughter, Miss Lorraine Grover, will be a débutante next winter." Also in 1927 came this note: "Mr. and Mrs. William D. Collins have sold their home at 5 Hortense place and have taken an apartment in the Greystone Apartments."

Just before the financial crash in September 1929, the sixteen-story Pierre Chouteau Apartment building at 4440 Lindell was under construction just opposite the

Advertisement for the Hampden Hall Apartments, southwest corner of McPherson and Newstead, *St. Louis Post-Dispatch* ad, 1925

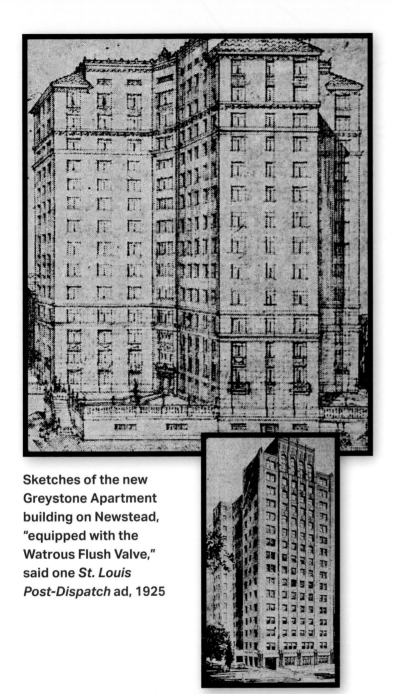

Sketches of the new Greystone Apartment building on Newstead, "equipped with the Watrous Flush Valve," said one *St. Louis Post-Dispatch* ad, 1925

New Cathedral. Its builder was Harry Felter, who had already constructed the President Apartments at 4615 Lindell. "Each apartment will be decorated with lead and oil paints in various color harmonies," said the announcement. "Property at 4426 and 4430 Lindell boulevard was recently acquired . . . and the houses are now being wrecked to make way for a playground more than two-fifths of an acre in area."

1927 TORNADO CUTS A SWATH OF DESTRUCTION

On Thursday, September 29, 1927, the barometer began falling, and around noon a powerful tornado suddenly touched down near Manchester and Kingshighway. Within minutes, it had devastated parts of the Central West End. Six workers were hurt and one killed at the Federal Motor Truck Company, 4022 West Pine, when a falling telegraph pole crushed the roof and the building collapsed. Another worker suffered head lacerations at the unroofed Brauer Brothers Shoe Company, Sarah and Forest Park. Two women were injured in their homes on the 4300 block of Laclede. One forty-nine-year-old man, William Fornoff, was walking into his home at 4222 McPherson when the building collapsed around him, but searchers couldn't find his body. "A small black dog to which Fornoff was attached and which he called

Left to right, **Photos of tornado destruction, 1927: Sarah and Easton; looking west on McPherson; 4201 Maryland where three women died; the Roselle Hotel, 4145 Lindell**

'Tiddles' stayed around one spot in the ruins. . . . Occasionally, he would paw the debris and bark. Under two feet of bricks, the body of Fornoff was unearthed," said one *Post-Dispatch* story, adding: "Lindell Boulevard, a main east-and-west traffic artery, was strewn with glass, shattered woodwork, poles, overturned automobiles and uprooted trees for a distance of eight blocks, between Sarah street and Euclid avenue. In some spots the wreckage covered the pavement to a depth of inches. Apparently the glass and woodwork had been blown from the residence. Many of them were left barren, not only of window panes, but of window frames and doors as well. . . . The section near the New Cathedral seemed to be the most seriously stricken."

A gas station in the 4000 block of West Pine collapsed, and a few blocks away on the same street "all the telegraph poles were snapped off like matches and the tops with crossarms were hurled in many places against the front of buildings and crashed through front windows and walls like battering rams," said the story. The beautiful Columbian Club was damaged, along with dozens of businesses and homes along a seven-mile path that stretched into Illinois.

One thousand army troops from Jefferson Barracks were dispatched to the city to help in the emergency.

Altogether, the storm leveled 460 houses, killed seventy-eight people in St. Louis, and injured more than five hundred others in only a few minutes. "Storm Is Most Deadly in St. Louis Since the Tornado of 1896," declared one *Post-Dispatch* headline, while the *Star* said, "City's Hospitals Filled with Injured After Storm," with twenty of the injured sent to Barnes.

ADVANCES AT BARNES, JEWISH, AND THE SCHOOL OF MEDICINE

During the 1920s and even the hard-pressed 1930s, the Washington University medical complex and the various hospitals in the neighborhood continued to expand. In 1930, Jewish Hospital dedicated a six-story nursing school building—a memorial to Moses Shoenberg, a founder of May Department Stores—at Kingshighway and Parkview Place. But two other planned buildings had to be postponed once the Depression began.

At the Washington University School of Medicine, surgery chairman Evarts Graham—who lived for years at 4711 Westminster in the Central West End, just down the block from W. McKim Marriott, chairman of pediatrics—saw that the increasingly distinguished radiology department deserved its own building. Joining him in the planning efforts were radiology chairman Sherwood Moore, seventy-five-year-old Robert Brookings, and even Abraham Flexner, now secretary of the Rockefeller-funded General Education Board, which promised an endowment if a donor would fund the building. Graham paid a visit to Edward Mallinckrodt, Brookings's friend and a university trustee since 1902, who agreed to supply the money. The new Mallinckrodt Institute

Shoenberg Memorial Training School for Nurses, 1929

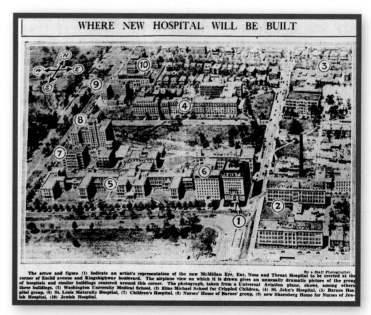

St. Louis Star, **June 13, 1929**

Edward Mallinckrodt Sr.
(1845–1928)

Mallinckrodt Institute of Radiology, c. 1931

Left to right, **Barnes Hospital buildings, St. Louis Maternity Hospital, McMillan Hospital, c. 1940**

of Radiology opened in 1931, though parts of it remained unfinished inside until financial conditions improved.

Other buildings came along, albeit with Depression-imposed economies. The Maternity Hospital went up in the mid-1920s and affiliated with Barnes Hospital in 1945. In 1929, the Rand-Johnson Memorial Surgical Building followed, funded mainly by International Shoe executives Frank Rand and Jackson Johnson, but it had to shrink to eight floors from the planned twelve. Eliza McMillan, who died in 1915, left her $1.5 million estate to build McMillan Hospital, starting in 1930. Along with these campus changes, the patient population was also growing rapidly, with 3,501 admitted to Barnes and its affiliated hospitals in 1920.

A MENAGERIE OF WRITERS

Popular writers were still cropping up along Central West End Streets. Poet and playwright Thomas Lanier ("Tennessee") Williams, briefly a Eugene Field School student and then a Washington University student in 1936, lived in a flat at 4633 Westminster Place, which he later described as "a perpetually dim apartment. . . . If we walked far enough west we came into a region of fine residences set in beautiful lawns. But where we lived, to which we must always return, were ugly rows of apartment buildings the color of dried blood and mustard." The family's building, now known as the "Glass Menagerie Apartments" after his play by that name, had a rear fire escape that must have inspired its opening scene. Best known for his Pulitzer Prize–winning play, *A Streetcar Named Desire*, Williams detested St. Louis. When he later returned to the university to give a talk, he said that his "only happy times . . . [in St. Louis] were at Washington University."

For part of his childhood, the family of novelist William Burroughs owned a house at 4664 Pershing, though they left for Ladue when he was twelve. But he still wrote about the Central West End. "In the 1920s, the United States, even the Midwest, was a place of glittering possibilities. You could be a gangster, a hard-drinking reporter, a jittery stock-broker, an expatriate, a successful writer. The possibilities spilled out in front of you like a rich display of merchandise. Sitting on the back steps drinking Whistle at twilight on a summer evening, hearing the street cars clang past on Euclid Avenue, I felt the excitement and nostalgia of the '20s. . . ."

In 1914, the poet Vachel Lindsay—whose most famous poem was "The Congo"—visited fellow poet Sara Teasdale

The childhood home of Tennessee Williams, known as the "Glass Menagerie Apartments"

William Burroughs (1914–1997) in 1965

Sara Teasdale, *St. Louis Post-Dispatch*, January 7, 1912

several times at her family's house at 38 Kingsbury Place, where she inhabited a restricted world, living in a suite of rooms upstairs and taking carriage rides in Forest Park. Lindsay, who had grown up in Springfield, Illinois, was in love with Teasdale but his visits—and his passionate love letters—didn't work. Later that year, she married businessman Ernst Filsinger, and Lindsay was crushed. After he committed suicide in 1931, she missed him; ironically, she ended her life the same way two years later.

Early in life, Irma von Starkloff Rombauer gave no hint that she would create the world-famous cookbook, *The Joy of Cooking*. She grew up in St. Louis as part of upper-middle-class German society, took art classes at Washington University, married Edgar Rombauer, joined with Edna Fischel Gellhorn in establishing a clinic to treat prostitutes for venereal disease, and in 1923 became president of the Wednesday Club. One of her children was Marion Rombauer, who married architect John Becker. But after Edgar's suicide, Irma needed to earn a living, and in 1931 she and Marion published their cookbook, which eventually became a best seller. Over the years, Irma lived at various Central West End locations, including an apartment at 5142 Waterman around 1925 and then one in the Monticello, 4605 Lindell, from 1955 to 1962.

Left, **Irma Rombauer (1877–1962)**

"NEGROES" NOT WELCOME

But this pleasant Central West End neighborhood was not open to everyone. In 1920, the *Post-Dispatch* published a story titled "Realty Exchange Opposes West End Sales to Negroes. . . . Section Specified Is Bounded by Grand Avenue, Kingshighway, Forest Park Bl. and Hodiamont Tracks." The Exchange board had voted unanimously on a resolution: "Any member of the Real Estate Exchange who sells or encourages the sale to negroes of property in [this] district . . . will be expelled from the exchange." They also endorsed the goals of the recently formed West End Protective Association "to block the threatened sale to negroes of a church at Enright and Newstead, and the reported negotiations for the sale of residences on that street to negroes." Why the opposition to black residents? The board agreed that "an incursion of negroes would 'shoot real estate values all to pieces' in that portion of the West End."

Exacerbating anti-black sentiment were newspaper articles about crime in the area with the race of the perpetrator highlighted. In 1930, a *Post-Dispatch* story reported, "William Green, clerk in a cigar store at 5616 Delmar boulevard, was firing the stove in the store yesterday when two negroes, one with a pistol, entered and commanded him to 'stick 'em up.' Green rushed at them. One picked up a

St. Louis Post-Dispatch, October 23, 1954

GROCER FIRES SHOTS AT FLEEING ROBBERS

Victim of $300 Holdup Says He Believes He Hit Auto of Two Men.

Jewell Boswell, a grocer, fired four pistol shots at two young men who held him up in his store, 4136 North Broadway, early today and fled with $300. He told police he thinks several shots struck the automobile in which the men drove north in Broadway.

Boswell said the men appeared a few minutes after he opened the store at 6:15 a.m., threatened him with revolvers and took his wallet containing the money. When they ran outside and started to drive away, Boswell grabbed his pistol from under the counter, ran to the door and fired.

Mrs. Henry Molos was standing near the cash register in her husband's market, 5204 Cates avenue, last night when a man entered, pressed a revolver against her back and demanded money. She gave him $300, and he fled west in Cates avenue. The robber was a Negro.

More than $1400 of the weekly payroll of Foster Bros. Manufacturing Co., 2101 South Vandeventer avenue, was taken yesterday by two men who slugged Mrs. Ralph Stricker, a bookkeeper, when she was returning to the office from a bank with the payroll. The robbers fled in an automobile parked near the office.

Mrs. Stricker, who was knocked down, was treated at St. John's Hospital for a head injury and shock. She lives at 4112 De-

length of gas pipe and smashed Green in the back of the head, knocking him senseless. When Green recovered consciousness 15 minutes later, he discovered the cash register had been looted of $20."

SIGNS OF TROUBLE

By the 1930s—and even earlier—there were signs of trouble for the Central West End. "Phew! Isn't That Smell Awful?" asked one *Post-Dispatch* headline in 1911, and the story blamed meatpacking and glue-producing plants. "Summer breezes which, as a rule, are from the south in St. Louis, often carry the smell from them into Washington, West Pine and Lindell boulevards . . . and other fashionable residence districts." Even Archbishop Glennon complained about the "packing house odors," while "Theodore Papin of 3765 Lindell boulevard said the odor is absolutely unbearable at times, and that from what he had heard the whole neighborhood from Grand avenue to Forest Park is afflicted by it."

A pall of smoke was also hanging over the area. In 1930, a *Post-Dispatch* editorial titled "Wake Up, St. Louis!" outlined the problem: "The damage that smoke is doing to St. Louis is shocking. In the exclusive private places of the West End, where residence property is most valuable, the For Sale signs are significant. . . . As long as we have smoke, the

View of the Civil Courts Building as smoke pollution blots out the sun at mid-day, November 11, 1939.

WAKE UP, ST. LOUIS!

There was in the Post-Dispatch yesterday a letter which was like a blast of fresh air through the St. Louis tunnel. The writer wanted to know why we do not use natural gas, thus solving the smoke problem and breaking the hold which monopoly has upon the gas supply of the community.

It is a fair question, and one that should be answered. The damage that smoke is doing to St. Louis is shocking. In the exclusive private places of the West End, where residence property is most valuable, the For Sale signs are significant. It is so all over the city. The people want to move out into the County. They want to get away from the smoke. They want to get away from the dirt. They want to breathe fresh air. It is not merely their property that is damaged by the smoke. It is also their health.

St. Louis Post-Dispatch, September 9, 1930

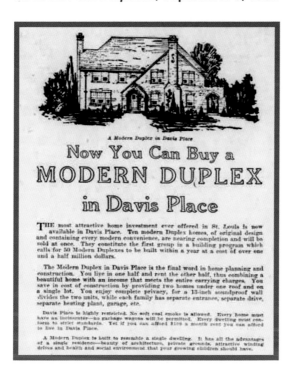

A Modern Duplex in Davis Place

Now You Can Buy a
MODERN DUPLEX
in Davis Place

St. Louis Post-Dispatch, August 30, 1925

Left, St. Louis chokes on smoke, November 11, 1939

exodus to the County will continue. The trees will die. The curtains will blacken. The house will be filthy. The health of the people will be bad." Ten years later, little had changed. In 1940, one *Post-Dispatch* headline read, "Smoke Blankets Much of City: 33rd Time in 96 Days," and continued, "In the West End for a time, tall buildings could not be distinguished more than about a block away."

In 1926, the Davis Realty Company began extolling the wonders of moving west to Davis Place in Clayton, calling it "the social and educational center in St. Louis. . . . Two minutes west of the millionaire colony of Brentmoor, Forest Ridge, and West Brentmoor." Among the attractions of Davis Place, they added, was that "you have no soft coal smoke, no garbage wagons. . . ."

Already, another exodus was beginning to the next stop in the residential migration westward. But what would happen to the area that the residents were leaving behind: the historic Central West End?

MILL CREEK VALLEY

View from Union Station of Mill Creek Valley prior to its demolition, 1959

CHAPTER 3

DESTRUCTION AND DECAY

A New Exodus to the West

(1940–1965)

"4378 Lindell Bl., 17 large rooms, 3 baths. Attractive interior, desirable for club, clinic, school, boarding house, rent $175 per month."

—Real estate ad, *St. Louis Post-Dispatch*, 1940

During the Depression, the secure world of the Central West End—peaceful, affluent, insular, and homogeneous—began to crumble under pressure from a multitude of forces. The financial slump made some of the large houses unaffordable. Afterwards, an array of plentiful, better-paying jobs made servants expensive and harder to find. Soon the wealthy, largely Protestant elite that had clustered on the private streets in 1912 began giving way to a more diverse, and dispersed, society. Suburban communities were burgeoning with lovely new homes. And improvements in transportation as well as roads put many of these neighborhoods, even in the distant suburbs, within easy reach. In 1945, for example, newspapers announced that Senator and Mrs. W. Stuart Symington, who had previously lived at 6 Lenox Place, had bought a new home on Ladue Road, west of Spoede.

After World War II, a frantic crush of returning veterans, many newly married, overwhelmed the housing market. Right away, that fixed the Central West End even more firmly in the sights of canny developers. With apartments at a premium, there was money to be made by splitting up mansions of the wealthy into flats or even rooming houses. When the prices of nearby homes tumbled on those streets where rooming houses were located, speculators could buy

W. Stuart Symington,
St. Louis Star-Times,
April 23, 1941

RESIDENCE AT 6 LENOX PLACE BOUGHT BY W. S. SYMINGTON

The residence at 6 Lenox place has been acquired by W. S. Symington, president of the Emerson Electric Co. from Pierre Loisel Papin.

The first floor consists of large living room, dining room, lavatory, kitchen and butler's pantry. There are four bedrooms and two baths on the second floor, and three bedrooms and bath on the third floor. The garage is in the rear of the premises.

The purchaser will take possession in the late summer or early fall. Mr. and Mrs. Papin have plans for the erection of a residence in St. Louis County.

A. T. and Whitelaw Terry represented the seller and Edward L. Bakewell, the purchaser in the negotiations. The purchase price was not disclosed.

St. Louis Post-Dispatch
May 7, 1939

these new houses all the more cheaply—and split them up too. "Washington, 4549, First time offered: 11 rooms made into 6 apartments . . . price $11,500," read one 1946 want ad.

Feelings ran high in the Central West End about this trend. In 1941, two men spoke at a public meeting about the proliferation of rooming houses. Thomas W. White, a lawyer living at 5244 Westminster, pointed out that "the total assessed value of homes on his block, where boarding houses are prohibited, is $379,000, while the same block on Washington boulevard, which includes several rooming houses, is only $247,000," reported the *Post-Dispatch*. A real estate broker from Clayton tried to argue that Westminster residents were too protective when White broke in,

heatedly: "He's destroyed Washington; now he wants to destroy Westminster!"

Some hotel owners also focused on boosting profits by chopping up their spaces. In an article titled "Day after Day, Thousands of Persons Here Continue Futile Search for Decent Place to Live," one newspaper reported that a West End hotel "told a house hunter they had cut their suites into single rooms, because they could make more money that way. When he asked about one of the permanent apartments, he was informed, without any mincing of words, that they were doing their best to get the tenants out of those, because then they could also cut them up into individual rooms and get as much as $100 a month more out of them."

But residents began to fight back. In 1942, individual property owners plus the Fullerton Place Association filed suit "to enjoin Arthur E. Hodges and Zovie Hodges from operating a boarding and rooming house at 4421 Westminster Place. . . . They allege that such use of the premises is contrary to the city zoning ordinance restricting property in the district for single family dwellings," said one newspaper story.

But oddly enough, at exactly the same time, some want ads reflected the old Central West End world, as if nothing had changed. In 1940, one ad called for a "Houseman, colored, with limited chauffeur service, steady job, West End." Another, in the same year, was looking for: "Butler: Thoroughly experienced, references required, good wages, location West End in city; state if white or colored."

MILL CREEK VALLEY SLUMS EMPTY OUT

By 1949, one of the most distressed areas in St. Louis was the Mill Creek Valley, a 327-acre area extending from Twentieth Street west to Grand, not far from the Central West End. In this area, which one newspaper story called "the city's No. 1 slum cancer," 20,000 people occupied 5,600

St. Louis Post-Dispatch: top, **November 25, 1945;** *bottom,* **May 4, 1956**

Left, **Sidney Maestre and Mayor Raymond Tucker on rooftop overlooking area of Mill Creek Valley slated for clearance, 1956.** *Middle,* **aerial view of Twenty-second and Scott looking north, c. 1930.** *Right,* **dilapidated buildings at 3526 Lawton with Grand Avenue skyline in background, 1961.**

homes; "89 percent are renter-occupied; 88 percent lack private baths, and 55 percent do not have running water. . . . About three-fourths of the residents are Negro. Overcrowding, defined as more than 1.5 persons per room, has been found in 25 percent of the units."

The Land Clearance for Redevelopment Authority declared the area blighted and unsanitary and said it "constitutes a serious and growing menace, injurious and inimical to the public health, safety, morals and welfare." The board of aldermen agreed. Rejecting the interest of a famous New York developer, the Authority turned the massive project over to a group that included St. Louis firms—"familiar personalities," sniffed the *Post-Dispatch*, "with a lack of broad-gauge,

long-term vision." But many also began to ask a crucial question: What would happen to the 4,200 families displaced by the slum clearance project?

Clearance began in 1960, with much of the vacated land reused for expressways, commercial purposes, or Saint Louis University expansion, and only a small piece rededicated to housing for the poor. Thus, most of the families swept away by the project had to find new homes in the area. Some moved west, especially to areas north of Delmar. Central West End residents complained about this influx to city officials, who denied that it was happening. "One inaccurate criticism that has been made," said Charles L. Farris, executive director of the St. Louis Land Clearance

"In the late 1950s and early 1960s, the city of St. Louis got involved in what at the time was called slum removal—urban renewal—and they concentrated on the Mill Creek Valley area. They bought people out and cleared the area.

"Mill Creek Valley was a deeply dysfunctional neighborhood. However, the real tragedy was that there were almost no relocation and displacement plans; some families went to housing projects such as Pruitt-Igoe, but others began a migration westward. And that migration of a very poor, predominantly black, population wound up devastating a lot of neighborhoods, in that central corridor. The Central West End was also under a tremendous amount of pressure during that period."

—Jerry King,
later director of the Washington University Medical Center
Redevelopment Corporation

Mill Creek Valley prior to its demolition, undated

and Housing Authority, in 1961, "is that families uprooted by the Mill Creek Valley redevelopment project flooded into the West End, overcrowding it. The fact is . . . that only 18 percent of the relocated Mill Creek families moved into the West End, with almost all of the remainder going into neighborhoods east and north of the West End." Still, even 18 percent translated into 3,600 people, placing new pressure on these streets.

Black residents also began moving into previously all-white parts of the Central West End. Some residents saw the area's decline, said a *Globe-Democrat* story, as relating directly to "an influx of people from the slums cleared out of the Mill Creek area." And white flight from all-white streets only accelerated as a result.

THE CENTRAL WEST END ASSOCIATION FORMS TO HELP

In 1955, the Central West End Neighborhood Improvement Association (later shortened to the Central West End Association) formed to fight encroaching urban blight. In a large meeting at the St. Louis Cathedral School that April, the association set up thirty block units, in an area bounded by Kingshighway, Boyle, West Pine, and Westminster, "to urge home-owners to improve their property by painting,

"In 1955–56, after I got back from the military, I was living in the neighborhood when I wandered in and discovered that, on Sunday evenings, Second Presbyterian Church had suppers for 65 cents for single adults. So I started coming to supper and to church services. It was an elegant, aristocratic church, and a lot of wealthy people were members. Some members came in chauffeured limousines, and the chauffeurs would sit in an anteroom next to the sanctuary, listening to the service.

"As some of the affluent members died or moved away, they were replaced by younger people, and the church changed focus, becoming very concerned about the neighborhood. Some houses nearby were being converted into illegal rooming houses. The church brought in consultants, and they identified several key properties that were bringing down the quality of life. One was an apartment house at the end of our block, where Tennessee Williams had lived when he was young. So the church formed a corporation called Christian Neighbors and, with financing from the federal government, bought the building, transformed it, and helped to change the character of the neighborhood.

"There was also a 'stroll' north of the church at Washington and Taylor. Some women in our church decided they would take down the license numbers of the cars going by, work with the police to find the drivers' home addresses, and send postcards that said: 'Your car was seen in an area of ill repute. Please don't come back.' We never knew who read the cards, but with that and several other police efforts, the area changed."

—Donald Beimdiek,
attorney and Second Presbyterian Church member

decorating, and landscaping. They also will be urged to maintain minimum housing standards and observe zoning regulations." Mayor Raymond Tucker attended, praising the "grass roots movement" and pledging the support of city agencies in this fight.

Soon the association, headed by Joseph McDonald, an investment broker who lived at 4515 Pershing, was taking on other neighborhood improvement battles: removing battered cars from the street, increasing street light wattage, promoting tree trimming, combating litter, and setting up a do-it-yourself program that encouraged owners to clean up their properties. In 1960, a junior auxiliary to the association, the City Slickers, mounted their own project, "A Can Can Do It," in which they decorated trashcans. Soon the association was holding such fundraisers as an annual City Living Tour, with houses on display including 1 Portland Place, owned by art collector Otto Erker; 46 Kingsbury Place, owned by Chapin Newhard; and 12 Hortense Place, owned by physician Hyman Fingert, who helped found the St. Louis Psychoanalytic Institute.

Other groups also began forming. A seven-congregation consortium—Trinity Episcopal, Second Presbyterian, St. Stephen's, First Unitarian, the St. Louis Cathedral, the Greek Orthodox church, and Temple Israel—pledged

Central West End Improvement Association Is Being Organized

An organization session has been called for 8 p.m. next Tuesday at the auditorium of the Cathedral School to complete development of a newly organized Central West End Improvement Association in St. Louis. Much preliminary work has been done, a preliminary organization being already in existence with Joseph B. McDonald of Reinholdt & Gardner, investment house, as interim chairman, and with a board of 25 trustees, made up of leading citizens in the area.

Property over which the association hopes to achieve a measure of maintenance and improvement guidance is that stretching from Boyle to Union boulevard and taking in, be-

dell, Maryland, Pershing, Mc-Pherson and Westminster place, together with whatever private places, may be within that area, whose trustees may wish to adhere to the policies and principles of the improvement association.

Not residences alone, but all investment and commercial property interests in the Central West End, will be urged to participate in order to preserve the area from decay and disintegration and [improvement] where pro[...] Enno [...] appraiser, chairman [...] mittee" to [...] the assoc[...] (after the [...]

St. Louis Post-Dispatch articles announcing community organization: *top*, April 10, 1955; *bottom*, June 27, 1962

CENTRAL WEST AREA SHOP, HOME OWNERS JOIN IN REJUVENATION

Euclid-McPherson Section Spurred by Spirit of Improvement — Buildings Being Modernized.

A new area is growing up in west central St. Louis, spurred partly by a spirit of neighborhood improvement, and partly by the wish of a handful of persons for a kind of urban quietude.

The nucleus of this growth is at the intersection of Euclid and McPherson avenues. Surrounding is an area brought to a standstill years ago by neighborhood stagnation. Now it is moving forward again on steady legs, said nearby residents and shop owners.

Flanked by Maryland Plaza on the south and Delmar boulevard to the north, Euclid-McPherson is a center of neighborhood rejuvenation. To many of the persons who have opened

Rehabilitated residence at 4632 McPherson Avenue, 1961

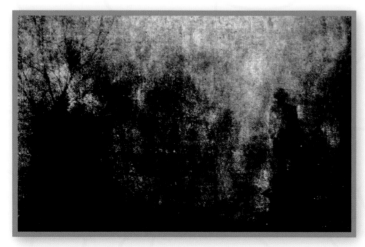

City hall at 9:30 in the morning blocked out by smoke pollution, November 28, 1939

in November 1955 to help fight blight. The director of education for Temple Israel suggested that the annual paint-up and clean-up parade by schoolchildren be routed through the district's blighted areas. He also urged new efforts to improve the neighborhood schools, which "are unsatisfactory and have caused a migration of desirable residents to the county."

The churches worked to create a more attractive social life among their members. In the late 1940s, Second Presbyterian and St. John's Methodist established young people's groups. "Apartment and hotel dwellers in the West End are particularly invited as are young couples 'temporarily' stuck in one room. They'll find others in the class with similar stories," said one notice.

SMOKE ABATEMENT WORKS

Amid much troubling news, one major piece of progress heartened residents in the early 1940s. Smoke pollution, produced by the burning of soft coal from Illinois mines by residents and businesses, had decidedly improved. No longer was the sky black with smoke, even in the daytime; no longer was furniture coated with fine black dust. After years of complaints from residents, the city had finally gotten serious about change in November 1939. An unprecedented stretch

THE MARY RYDER HOME

In 1932, the Mary Ryder Home—named for Mary Elizabeth Ryder, a welfare activist and leader of the Typographical Union, who had founded the shelter two years earlier—began operating, quietly but effectively, at 3828 Westminster under the auspices of the Joint Council of Women's Auxiliaries Welfare Association. At its opening, the home was intended to accommodate eighteen to twenty girls or women who were making less than $10 per week and provide them with room and board for $3 a week.

Later, one more home opened at 4360 Washington and a third "for colored women" at 3534 Lawton. Today, the home, which has moved to 4361 Olive, is a residential care facility for low-income seniors.

Mary Ryder, *St. Louis Post-Dispatch* **December 15, 1932**

of nine hazy days had culminated in the infamous "Black Tuesday" of November 8, 1939, when cars had to use their headlights all day long and streetlights stayed on around the clock.

Raymond Tucker, a mechanical engineering professor at Washington University, was the hero of the reform efforts. As smoke commissioner, he pushed for the use of hard coal or other "smokeless fuel." The board of aldermen passed a new smoke elimination bill in April 1940. Some residents feared the higher cost of new fuel. Outside the aldermanic meeting was a truck bearing the sign: "New Coal Smoke at Higher Prices." But Tucker enforced the smoke ordinance wisely and well. "Mr. Tucker has a reputation for accomplishment," said a 1951 *Post-Dispatch* editorial. "His outstanding achievement in public service was his contribution to cleaning up the smoke evil between 1937 and 1941."

The prestige that Tucker gained from his public service helped him win the mayor's office in 1953, 1957, and 1961, though he was defeated for a fourth term in the Democratic primary by Alfonso Cervantes. In 1944, the *Post-Dispatch* won a Pulitzer Prize in Public Service for its "successful campaign against city smoke nuisance."

PERSHING BECOMES A "PLACE"

As early as 1951, residents of Pershing just east of Euclid were becoming concerned about their street. A run-down building on Euclid near Maryland was on the verge of becoming a nursing home, and trucks often sped down the two-block stretch where dozens of children lived. In 1955, Joseph McDonald, who had moved to the street in 1950 and was then president of the Pershing Avenue Improvement Association, spurred residents to action. They filed a request with the Board of Public Service to establish those two blocks as a private place, "designed to maintain property values and block blight and decay," said one account.

At a hearing, one hundred residents of the area attended and spoke in favor of the proposal. "In view of the rebirth of St. Louis as a progressive city," said Sylvan Agatstein, attorney for the residents, "it is important that this nucleus of prominent residents be kept intact. These people should be encouraged to stay in the city rather than move to St. Louis

ONE HOMEOWNER REFUSES TO GIVE IN

In 1961, the *Globe-Democrat* praised the efforts of one Central West End property owner, Raymond Loos, who was working to "put a new face on the 4200 block of Maryland Avenue." Five years earlier, Loos had bought a handsome brick home at 4225 Maryland and "spent every spare minute working on his property. He sifted the dirt in the back yard down to a depth of 4 inches and produced what looks like a big putting green." He joined the Central West End Association "and started trying to get something done about cluttered alleys and broken sidewalks." Then he bought the home next door at 4229 Maryland, renovated it, and rented it.

His efforts seemed to be contagious. Along his block, twelve other houses received fresh coats of paint within two months. "A number of uneven, dangerous sidewalk sections are being replaced. Trees are trimmed and neat," said the story.

"'We've got to keep the filth cleaned up,' said Loos, an automobile production worker, "speaking intensely as he gazed at the vacant house across the street." Added a city official: "Something has been accomplished in Mr. Loos's neighborhood that should spread to other areas."

Left, **11 Westmoreland Place, undated;** *right,* **4487 Lindell, undated.**

County." The board agreed. In October 1956, new entrance columns at both ends of the two-block span were in place and that section of Pershing had become a private street, renamed Pershing Place.

BUILDINGS COME . . . AND GO

"St. Louis' 'dowager' Central West End used to be like an old lady grown frowzy with age. But now, in spots of that section of once-stately homes, the dowdy dowager looks more like a delightful debutante," read a cheerful *St. Louis Globe-Democrat* story in 1956. "Shabby mansions have been done over, to become sleekly sophisticated town houses." One example, said the article, was the 300 block of Walton, where there were six townhouses in a row with charming gardens out back. Another was

the 4300, 4400, and 4500 blocks of Maryland, which had "new paint, new brasswork, new greenery." And another story, in 1961, touted the area's redevelopment efforts, totaling $15 million in the 183-block Central West End neighborhood. "Behind the statistics lies one example after another of a drab corner brightened, a shabby residence remodeled, a helter-skelter of unwanted buildings replaced by a new structure," said one *Globe-Democrat* story.

But not everything was so rosy. After years of vacancy, the once-glorious Samuel Kennard mansion at 4 Portland Place came down in 1958. Two years later, Lindell lost five historic houses from its 4400 block, among them 4499, the home of milling firm head E. O. Stanard, and 4475, once occupied by James Cahill, who helped found the St. Louis Stock Exchange. Two mansions across the street were razed for construction of the Optimist Club International building. "Houses such as these," wrote Norbury Wayman, "contained as many as sixteen rooms with grand staircases and oversized halls. Paneled living rooms, bedrooms with fireplaces, marble bathrooms, and servants' quarters in these houses were symbolic of an opulent by-gone era." While houses were sometimes torn down for new construction, he added, another reason "influencing demolition . . . was economic; that is, razing to save taxes and maintenance costs."

Also in 1960, the south side of West Pine lost twelve historic houses, which were replaced by apartment buildings. That left only five of the original houses standing, including the stunning Butler House, 4484 West Pine, built in 1892 in the Queen Anne style for tobacco executive James Gay Butler. After he died in 1916, the house was sold to Grace Cain, but by the 1950s it was a rooming house, though it managed to survive demolition.

Top, **Washington University Medical School, c. 1957;** *above,* **St. Louis Star-Times, August 22, 1916,** *right,* **residence at 4499 Lindell, undated**

THE HISTORY OF A CENTRAL WEST END HOUSE: 4335 WEST PINE

At 4335 West Pine on the corner of Boyle once stood a stately mansion whose fate mirrored that of the Central West End during the early to mid-twentieth century. In 1900, this fourteen-room mansion was the home of William H. ("Colonel") Swift, a leading Democrat, former newspaper publisher, and president of Fruin-Bambrick Construction Co. This general contracting firm owned several quarries in the St. Louis area.

But Swift, a widower, died in 1915 at age eighty-three, and his funeral was held in the New Cathedral. Afterward, his house fell into other hands, and by 1929 it was for sale, along with other large homes nearby: 4047 West Pine (nine rooms), 4131 West Pine (fourteen rooms) 4324 Maryland (eleven rooms). "Any one of the above can be bought on reasonable terms and at a real bargain," said a Glick Realtors ad. Another 1929 notice called the home "suitable for a rooming house."

In 1934, the home was advertised again as a building containing "small apartments" for rent. One of them was occupied by Mrs. Frances Carroll, a worker at the National Underwear Corporation, Boyle and Duncan, where two hundred women employees had been on strike for a month, "joined in their picketing by divinity students, socially prominent women and sympathizers from garment unions," said one newspaper account. But Carroll was a nonstriker and her scuffle with a striker made the papers.

The mansion was again for sale in 1943, and its small apartments seemed to be attracting a less desirable clientele. In 1952, one resident was sentenced to thirty days in the workhouse for driving while intoxicated and leaving the scene of an accident.

Vignette

By 1955, black families were living in the building, now a rooming house. "Falling Cabinet Kills 3-Year-Old," read one heartbreaking headline. Little Walter Slinger Jr., a three-year-old, mischievously tried to climb up a large china cabinet in an unoccupied room when the heavy piece of furniture fell on him. He was taken to Homer G. Phillips Hospital, where he was pronounced dead.

In 1964, a newspaper story noted that, "Post Plaza Savings and Loan Association, 1800 Olive street, has arranged a $50,000 loan for the construction of a nursing home at 4335 West Pine Boulevard. This home, Fountain House, Inc., is planned to accommodate 104 patients." The nursing home, "named for a large fountain on the front lawn which will be illuminated by soft-colored changeable lights," was finished in 1965.

Within a few years, the home was renamed the Bernard West Pine Care Center, and today it is the Bernard Care Center, part of a nursing home group.

WATCH FOR OPENING SOON!

FOUNTAIN HOUSE INC.

Professional Nursing Home in a Luxurious Hotel Setting

4335 WEST PINE BLVD.

The Fountain House is locally owned and administered. For the retired, convalescent and patients who require skilled care.

RESERVATIONS NOW BEING **ACCEPTED**

CALL
MRS. EVELYN STONE, RN. **JE 1-2663**

Fountain House, 1965

One of its residents in 1980 was Edwina Dakin Williams, mother of playwright Tennessee Williams. She had previously lived at the Gatesworth Manor, 245 Union Boulevard. Edwina Williams, who died at the home after living there for about a year, may have been the inspiration for the mother, Amanda Wingfield, in *The Glass Menagerie.*

**Edwina Dakin Williams
in a 1974 photo**

In 1963, Glick Real Estate built the 48-unit Pierre Laclede Apartments at 5438 Delmar. And a new fifteen-story Lindell Terrace apartment building, designed by Hellmuth, Obata + Kassabaum (HOK), went up on Lindell at Taylor. "Large glare and heat-resistant grey glass windows will provide views from each of the apartments," said a newspaper description. The $5 million building, the "first major St. Louis building to be completed in the city's Bicentennial year," was officially opened by Mayor Raymond Tucker and builder Alvin Siteman.

Other buildings constructed during the mid-1960s included the St. Louis de Ville Motor Hotel, the Chancery Archdiocese building, and the Executive House Apartments. These latter apartments advertised themselves as "St. Louis' tallest and most select apartment building—24 floors of magnificence—with an address in the 'preferred' part of the city."

TWO HOTELS AND MORE FOR SAM

Patiently, Sam Koplar—who had lost his beloved Park Plaza in the Depression—was waiting for the right moment to make his move, and it came in November 1944. The holding company that owned the Park Plaza was tired of owning it and ready to make a deal. With the help of his brother Harry, a financial whiz, Sam presented an offer of $3 million, and the company accepted it. So Sam had his cherished

Construction of the Lindell Terrace Apartments, 1963.

Sam Koplar, *St. Louis Star-Times*, April 1, 1942

"My father was very concerned at one point because the wrong element was moving into the neighborhood. When the Saks building became empty, there was a big hole in what this area could be and should be. Do you remember that in the early '70s there was a bombing where Straub's Market is? My father decided that the Chase Park Plaza was such a big entity for the city that we should come up with a plan for Maryland Plaza. Mayor Al Cervantes and my father came up with a plan for the street. It turned out to be OK, not great—but an improvement. I think the neighbors didn't quite accept the cobblestone streets in place at the time."

—Ted Koplar,
son of Harold Koplar, owner of the Chase Park Plaza

hotel back for a bargain price. "Nobody knew it the way I did, and nobody could run it as well as I could," he said later. Two years later to the day, he gained majority control of the Chase Hotel—a victory made all the sweeter by the hotel's early reputation for anti-Semitism. He and Jeannette moved to the seventeenth floor of the Park Plaza, and he continued to groom their son Harold, already serving as manager of the Forest Park Hotel, as his replacement.

Harold, a former architecture student, loved to design and try novel things, and the Chase Hotel gave him scope. In 1940, a gala evening marked the opening of a new venue, designed by Harold: the tenth-floor Starlight Roof and adjacent Zodiac Cocktail Lounge. In the Zodiac Lounge, a dazzling circular glass bar had the twelve signs of the zodiac etched into its surface. In

the middle was the silver figure of a girl pointing up to a dome that slid open to reveal the sky. Increasingly, Harold also booked acts for the popular Chase Club, including such big names as the Dorsey brothers, Dean Martin and Jerry Lewis, Guy Lombardo, Sophie Tucker, and the Freddy Martin band with a young Merv Griffin. Occasionally, there were acts that didn't pan out. "We had more bombs than Berlin," sighed Harold once.

After the war, Harold Koplar took over as vice president and general manager of the Chase, Park Plaza, Forest Park, Branscome, and Embassy Hotels—the biggest hotel group in St. Louis. In 1953, he bought the Chester Apartments on Lindell and in 1956 added the adjoining Chase Apartments. And he continued to innovate, developing the Tiara Room on the twenty-seventh floor of the Park Plaza, a new swimming pool

Veiled Prophet Ball in the Khorassan Room, *St. Louis Post-Dispatch*, October 2, 1957

Scene from the Khorassan Room in the early 1960s, *St. Louis Post-Dispatch*, November 5, 1999

for the Chase in 1953, and the Khorassan Room in 1957. This huge, opulent ballroom was inaugurated in a glittering "Spirit of St. Louis" Ball, a fundraiser for the Missouri Historical Society, with Guy Lombardo's band providing entertainment. At the end of the 1950s, Koplar designed an expanded lobby and hallway, lined with exclusive shops, that tied the Park Plaza and Chase together.

The Chase Park Plaza was becoming a self-contained city, with its own upholstery and decorating shop, printing office, giant laundry, maintenance and security operations, and basement pastry department. Meanwhile, the hotel became a key stopping-off place for major league baseball teams; celebrity entertainers such as Robert Goulet and Carol Lawrence, Lena Horne, Nat King Cole, Harry Belafonte, and Danny Thomas; and also political figures, including US presidents Franklin Roosevelt, Harry Truman, Dwight Eisenhower, John Kennedy, Lyndon Johnson, Richard Nixon, Ronald Reagan, and Jimmy Carter. The entertainment side of the Chase, which hosted such traditional society events as the Veiled Prophet Ball, was also changing. One surprisingly successful idea from Harold was *Wrestling at the Chase*, a campy mix of brawn and elegance, held in the posh Khorassan Room.

In 1959, a new independent television station began to broadcast in St. Louis, making its headquarters in the Chase Apartments building. KPLR–TV 11 was Harold Koplar's latest brainchild, but it needed imaginative programming. Soon, in a pact he made with August A. ("Gussie") Busch Jr., he snagged the Cardinals baseball games. He also began airing *The Three Stooges*, which made a hit with kids. Then he signed Harry Fender, a resident of the Park Plaza, to headline *Captain 11's Showboat*, starting in 1960.

ANOTHER TORNADO DAMAGES THE CENTRAL WEST END

In February 1959, another twister hit St. Louis—"worst storm in 32 years," screamed one headline. In all, nineteen people were killed, three hundred were injured, and nearly two thousand buildings were damaged. Touching down in Crestwood and Brentwood, the storm moved on toward Forest Park, forging a "Path of Destruction in Central St. Louis," said the story. There were casualties in the 4300 block of McPherson and 4200 block of Delmar, but some of the worst devastation took place at the corner of Delmar and Whittier, where at least eight people were killed in one demolished building.

St. Louis Post-Dispatch, September 3, 1961.

ST. LOUIS POST-DISPATCH FINAL

19 KILLED AS TORNADO HITS HERE

300 INJURED IN WORST STORM IN 32 YEARS

1725 HOMES, BUSINESS BUILDINGS DAMAGED

Left, *St. Louis Post-Dispatch*, February 10, 1959; *upper right,* house at 4214 Washington minus roof and windows, February 11, 1959; *lower right,* view of the 4200 block of Olive at Boyle showing damage to a building with restaurants and apartments

"On the grounds of the Academy of the Sacred Heart, nuns moved about, singly and in groups, trying to determine the damage that had been done to their school," said a *Post-Dispatch* story. The area around the academy, at Maryland and Taylor, was hard hit by the storm. "Huge trees had been torn from the ground, their naked roots lying exposed. . . . The two huge stained-glass windows which were the pride of the school and the chief adornment of the chapel, had been blown to bits. 'But we were fortunate,' one of the nuns said, 'Nobody was hurt. In that building over there, I understand, two men died.' She was pointing to a heating plant back of McAuley Hall, which is on the next street. A tall brick smoke stack had gone over on the building, almost crushing it to the ground. Two men had been killed."

Pieces of the front wall of the Westmoreland Hotel at Taylor and Maryland had fallen into its front yard exposing furniture inside that was eerily untouched. The sculptor Carl Mose, who lived on Maryland, awoke to find his back fence "uprooted, torn apart, and piled together in the middle of [his garden]." At Olive and Boyle, in a young arts and entertainment district called Gaslight Square, the tornado wrought havoc with buildings. "The Golden Eagle, in the heart of the district, looked at first glance as though it had been bombed. . . . The Gaslight, another tavern around the corner on Boyle Avenue, lost its front door. On the bar were the remains of a dozen highballs, which gave the impression the place had been vacated in a hurry. . . ."

Gaslight Square in 1961: *Top left,* Insomniac Coffee House. *Bottom left,* the Laughing Buddha, 461 North Boyle. *Right,* Gaslight saloon, 457 North Boyle.

St. Louis Post-Dispatch ads for Gaslight Square: 1962 (*above*) and 1965 (*below*)

"A CHARMING REFUGE": GASLIGHT SQUARE

As the tornado struck, Gaslight Square was just getting off the ground. "As many St. Louisans know, plans for renovating the Olive-Boyle area were just beginning to materialize," wrote Jay Landesman, producer and rehabilitation committee member. "This week's disaster has increased our determination to continue with the project of developing this historic little section for reuse as a charming refuge for St. Louisans."

In Gaslight Square, said a news story, buildings were decorated with "castoff fragments decreed worthless and wrecked in land-clearance projects. The salvagers blew the dust off the wrought iron, cut stone, handsomely tailored wood, gas lights and old brick literally pulled from junk piles." In 1963, Laclede Gas Co. installed one hundred old-fashioned gas lamps in the area so that it would live up to its name.

At its height, the area drew visitors to some fifty attractions, including the Crystal Palace cabaret theater at 4240 Olive, co-owned by Landesman; the Carriage House, Kotobuki, Magnolia House, and Three Fountains restaurants; the Natchez Queen, created to look like a riverboat and offering ragtime music; a theater in the round; jazz venues; antique shops; and art exhibitions in summer. One shop, Spot on the Square, displayed paintings from such St. Louis artists as Howard Jones and Leslie Laskey. The Laughing Buddha Coffee House featured "America's finest folk singers," including Peter Yarrow. The Crystal Palace was particularly exciting, showcasing such new talent as the Smothers Brothers and Barbra Streisand, "who shows considerable promise," said one review.

But some articles also detailed crimes in the neighborhood and asked whether Gaslight Square was really as chic as it pretended. "What is Gaslight Square? It is a grotesque section of the city where excess-profit seekers capitalize on suburbanite escapism," said a cheerless *Post-Dispatch* letter writer in 1961.

LOCAL BUSINESSES AND THE "FIFTH AVENUE OF ST. LOUIS"

A little further east was a St. Louis landmark: Ben J. Selkirk & Sons Auctioneers, where weekly furniture auctions offered consigned items from estates and business liquidations. In 1931, Selkirk's had moved from the Arcade Building to a two-story, 15,000-square-foot headquarters at 4517–19 Olive. In 1936, it moved to 4166 Olive at Whittier, and it did so well that the business expanded in 1938 to the adjacent

Newspaper ad for Ben J. Selkirk & Sons, 1936

Newspaper ads for Maryland Avenue stores: 1942 (*above*) and 1948 (*below*)

building on the east. One Selkirk regular was Sam Koplar, who attended every Tuesday furniture auction to find bargains for his hotels. The Chase Park Plaza truck would follow him and carry his purchases back to the hotels, where he stored them in the capacious basements.

By the 1940s, Maryland Plaza had developed a thriving commercial district. Occupying one of the buildings on the plaza was Montaldo's, a high-end women's store that opened in 1941 and expanded to a two-story, 20,000-square-foot space in 1947. Josephine Scullin Dresses was around the corner at 387 North Euclid. Swope's Shoes was at 4663 Maryland, while Lockhart's Inc. was at 4926 Maryland. Other businesses—Leppert-Roos Furs and the Avenue Shop ("where Discriminating Women Buy Dresses, Gowns and Accessories")—added to the mix. A later retailer was Saks Fifth Avenue, which moved into the vacated Lockhart's space in 1956 and attracted a well-to-do clientele. Ads promoted the Oleg Cassini resort collection or Mollie Parnis designs. In 1948, ads called Maryland Plaza, perhaps a bit too optimistically, the "5th Avenue of St. Louis . . . Exclusive . . . but never Expensive."

Another shop that opened in 1949 and remained in the Central West End until 2003 when it moved to Maplewood was Norton's Fine Art and Framing, owned by Doug Norton and his wife, Mary. They initiated the "gallery walks" that often took place on Sundays in concert with fashion shows sponsored by the elite fashion retailers in the area. "It all stemmed from [the Central West End] being the shopping area. It had a cosmopolitan, New York air to it," said Doug Norton.

By 1956, police were fed up with inconsiderate women shoppers, especially in the 4900 block of Maryland, who double- or even triple-parked on the busy thoroughfare. "Shoppers . . . Hop Out and Run into Specialty Stores There," read a disapproving headline. The entrance to the Park Plaza was often blocked and traffic backed up onto Kingshighway. "Parking is bad enough on Maryland," said one customer, "but there are other things that go on in the block that make the traffic situation even worse. Some drivers window-shop from their cars, and others love to make U-turns in the middle of the block."

Another business to arrive in the Central West End was the popular Straub's grocery store at Maryland and Kingshighway, built in the 1940s. Already, Straub's had locations in Webster Groves and Clayton. The new site was popular enough that in 1948 Straub's wanted to grow, but the Park Plaza across the street protested that this expansion would violate city zoning restrictions. The *Post-Dispatch* noted archly that the head of the board of adjustment, which had

St. Louis Post-Dispatch article subtitled "Police to Crack Down on Double Parking by Women on Maryland," December 16, 1956

Corner Opposite The Park Plaza Leased 50 Years

St. Louis Post-Dispatch, July 14, 1946

William A. Straub & Co., which operates three large food markets in St. Louis suburbs, will have its first store inside the city limits early next year. Property at the northeast corner of Kingshighway and Maryland avenue, opposite the Park Plaza Hotel, has been leased for 50 years as site of the new operation.

The property, numbered 302 North Kingshighway, and 4969 Maryland, is owned by the Rookery Realty, Loan, Investment & Building Co., and has been leased by the Parkside Realty Co., holding agency for the Straub company.

Walter A. Straub, who signed the lease for Parkside, said the new store will have about 8000

The Salad Bowl Restaurant, September 16, 1962

River des Peres
drainage project, 1929

approved the Straub's application, was the same man hired to make the alterations.

Restaurants also made their appearance, such as the Majestic, which opened in 1960 and added a cocktail lounge in 1977. In 1964, the Majestic won honorable mention in a contest sponsored by the Missouri Restaurant Association that attracted more than five hundred entries. The Chase Park Plaza Hotel won first prize in the cakes category for its famous strawberry cheesecake. Another popular Central West End restaurant, the Salad Bowl Cafeteria—which had moved to a new location at 3949 Lindell in 1962 from an earlier spot at 4057 Lindell, where it had been since 1951—also won a first prize for its noted chiffon pie.

CHANGES IN FOREST PARK

Through these years, Forest Park had undergone major changes. In 1923, a large bond issue was on the ballot that would provide funds to submerge the dirty, smelly River des Peres, which snaked its way through the park and nearby neighborhoods. In their book on Forest Park, Caroline Loughlin and Catherine Anderson quoted from a billboard in the park that read: "Think this over. What other Big City would have an open sewer running through a fine big Park? Henry W. Kiel Mayor." Not surprisingly, the measure passed overwhelmingly. The river was forced underground for much of its course through the city, including the nearby Skinker-DeBaliviere neighborhood.

New attractions had grown up in the park, such as the open-air Municipal Opera (or Muny) in 1919; new greenhouses; a charming bandstand donated by lawyer Nathan Frank in 1925; a new Jewel Box conservatory—"the last word in display greenhouses," said the *Post-Dispatch*—in 1936; two new waterfalls; and new rose gardens. Existing park attractions, such as the zoo, also expanded, and the Muny added a new entrance in 1940. In the postwar years, the park was well used, though vandalism and theft, even of park plantings, was on the rise.

The major cultural institutions in the park were also growing, as the Saint Louis Art Museum added a large mezzanine in 1962, and the zoo attracted famed *Wild Kingdom* host Marlin Perkins as its head in the same year. When one of the zoo's favorite residents, Phil the Gorilla, died in 1958, they had him stuffed, mounted, and put on display. One piece of a 1955 city bond issue was $1 million for the construction of a planetarium, which went up on the site of the demolished Mounted Police Station, along the southern edge of the park. In 1964, it was named the McDonnell Planetarium in honor of major donor James S. McDonnell, founder of McDonnell Aircraft Corporation. And in 1957, the Mark C. Steinberg Memorial Skating Rink opened on a site near Kingshighway.

Top left, the Muny in Forest Park, 1946; *middle left,* bird cage repairs at the zoo, February 13, 1934; *middle right,* Forest Park Highlands roller coaster, "The Comet," at dusk, 1960; *bottom left,* World's Fair Pavilion in Forest Park, c. 1935; *right,* sleds and toboggans in Forest Park, 1947

Top left, Jefferson Memorial Building and intersection of Lindell and DeBaliviere after completion of the River des Peres drainage project, 1930; *bottom left,* Phil the Gorilla at the Saint Louis Zoo, undated; *right,* Saint Louis Art Museum, 1946.

Construction work on the Cancer Research Building, 1950

A view down Kingshighway, 1960

WASHINGTON UNIVERSITY GROWS

The postwar era ushered in a new period of expansion for Washington University, both on its main campus and at its medical school. The Depression-era belt-tightening was over, and the university grew along with the national economy. During the war, Lucille and Wallace Renard donated money for a neuropsychiatry department, and a bereaved David Wohl Sr. honored the memory of his son, a bombardier who died in action over Berlin, by funding construction of the David P. Wohl, Jr., Memorial Hospital and the David P. Wohl, Jr.–Washington University Clinics Building. In 1948, the Barnard Free Skin and Cancer Hospital affiliated with the school of medicine and later built a five-story building on campus.

The university also managed to snag an eminent scientist as chancellor: Arthur Holly Compton, a key figure in the Manhattan Project and a former faculty member at Washington University. With his own 1927 Nobel Prize in Physics, he joined a small group of other faculty members who were also Nobel laureates: Carl and Gerty Cori (1947) and Joseph Erlanger (1944). Thanks to his wartime credentials, Compton was able to attract chemists from the Manhattan staff, as well as a young environmentalist, Barry Commoner, who famously studied nuclear fallout. Other extraordinary scientists joined the faculty too, including ophthalmologist Bernard Becker, later a Central West End resident.

In 1953, the university welcomed a new chancellor, Ethan Shepley, a graduate of Smith Academy and Washington University School of Law with deep roots in the Central West End. Then in 1962, Shepley stepped down and was replaced by former Massachusetts congressman Thomas Eliot. The early 1960s was a period of upheaval at the school of medicine, in which Barnes board chairman Edgar Queeny and medical dean Edward Dempsey fought bitterly. To help defuse this crisis, the medical school created a new position—vice president for medical affairs, held from 1964 to 1965 by Carl Moore, respected head of internal medicine. In years to come, the occupants of this post would be vital to the university's intervention in its struggling neighborhood.

WESTWARD HO, AGAIN

Despite some positive signs in the neighborhood, some hospitals had had enough. A number moved away from the Central West End, and some built new "Palaces on Ballas," as outsiders wryly called them. Shriner's Hospital on South Euclid departed in 1963; so did St. John's, also on South Euclid, in the same year, and the building was demolished in 1967. Missouri Baptist, formerly on North Taylor, moved in

Aerial photo of the Washington University Medical Center campus, c. 1964

Aerial view of Queeny Tower construction, c. 1963

Shriner's Hospital, 700 South Kingshighway, 1946

Washington University Medical Center campus, looking south, 1964

1965, while St. Luke's, a mainstay on Delmar Boulevard, laid the cornerstone of its Chesterfield location in 1972.

That left Barnes, St. Louis Children's, and the Washington University School of Medicine clustered on their Kingshighway campus. Jewish Hospital was not far away at 216 South Kingshighway. The St. Louis College of Pharmacy, founded in 1864, which had moved from its downtown locations to Parkview Place and Euclid in 1927, was also staying. So was the pioneering Central Institute for the Deaf, founded in 1914 by otolaryngologist Max Goldstein. Its deaf education teacher-training program had affiliated with Washington University in 1931. Saint Louis University also remained at its South Grand location.

With the pressure of this rush westward, Washington University had to make a historic decision that would have extraordinary implications for its Central West End neighborhood, as well as the Forest Park Southeast neighborhood immediately to the south. Stay or go? And if they stayed, how could they help their troubled urban area?

CENTRAL WEST END DETERIORATION

A house is demolished along McPherson, 1967.

CHAPTER 4

HITTING BOTTOM AND COMING BACK

(1965–1975)

"If you can't save [the Central West End], what can you save in the city?"

—Elmer Smith,
regional director of the
US Department of Housing and Urban Development (HUD),
quoted in the *St. Louis Post-Dispatch*, March 5, 1972

The departure of nearly all the hospitals from the Central West End was just the beginning. From the mid-1960s on, the neighborhood suffered one loss after another—in residents, businesses, schools, even congregations—as the westward flight continued. On Kingsbury Place, for example, wrote Julius Hunter in his history of that street: "There were over forty transactions during which Kingsbury Place homes changed hands during the 1960s."

In an April 1972 *Post-Dispatch* article, city planners spoke bluntly about the continuing white flight from the city. "Another factor in the abandonment of the city has been the influx of blacks. From a 6 per cent black population in 1900 and 29 per cent in 1960, the city now has at least 41 per cent blacks," said the story. While the broader West End—north of Delmar and west of Union to Skinker—was most affected by the loss of white residents, the Central West End also felt the impact. "Call it prejudice, racism or ignorance: the fact remains that many persons left because they didn't want black neighbors," said the story.

The high-end shopping district on Maryland Plaza fell into a steep decline. Saks left for Plaza Frontenac in 1974; so did Montaldo's in 1975. Mermod, Jaccard & King Jewelry Co., which had opened at 50 Maryland Plaza in 1965, closed

St. Louis Post-Dispatch, May 21, 1974

Then there is Maryland Plaza, a hotbed of gossip and rumors about which shops are leaving and which are staying. A severe blow was dealt, at least symbolically, by the recent departure of Saks Fifth Avenue. But other commercial enterprises have moved into the area recently, including the Maryland Avenue Screening Room, a restaurant-movie theater operated by Alfonso J. Cervantes Jr.

ARCHITEC'S SKETCH of Montaldo's store that is to be opened in August at Plaza Frontenac Shopping Center, Lindbergh Boulevard and Clayton Road.

Saks (1970) and Montaldo's (1975) plan their moves west, from the *St. Louis Post-Dispatch*.

eight years later. Peck & Peck, Doubleday Bookstores, and Block Gallery also shut their doors, while the Woman's Exchange moved to Ladue in 1974, with one volunteer saying, "every comment we get from our older customers, telling us that we're deserting them, hurts us. We're not deserting them. It's a case of our consignors being hurt by the decline in business we now face in this area." The black-owned Fashion Palace burned down, amid whispers of arson. Parents in the area were devastated when City House and Barat Hall schools closed in 1967. The venerable Wednesday Club moved to Ladue in 1973. Even

churches were moving. As early as 1958, Second Baptist Church had left Holy Corners for a new Clayton and McKnight location. Four years later, Temple Israel dedicated its new sanctuary, designed by Gyo Obata, at Ladue and Spoede Roads, leaving behind its old synagogue at Holy Corners. The deeply divided congregation of Second Presbyterian Church came close to moving—first to Ladue and then to a lot at Lindell and DeBaliviere—but when the congregation voted, the decision to leave the neighborhood failed by only eleven votes.

Clockwise from far left: 4900 Washington, undated; Central West End street, undated; sidewalk damage, Forest Park at Euclid, April 1979; Lindell Plaza Hotel, 1975; Central West End street, undated

City Bank ad, *St. Louis Post-Dispatch,* **January 10, 1971**

Left, **aerial photo of Forest Park, the Washington University Medical Center, and the Central West End, c. 1973**

Crime was a constant worry, particularly along Delmar, DeBaliviere, and Pershing. But others, even in the heart of the neighborhood, were hit. "There was a funny story on Westminster Place," said resident Robert Duffy. "A friend told me his bicycle had been stolen, and I said, 'Big deal! That's an afternoon activity here.' Then he said, 'Yes, but they stole it from the room I was sitting in.' So it was not good. There were regular break-ins and daytime robberies; people were fearful to go out at night and walk the dog. Forest Park was considered the scariest place in the world."

In November 1973, a front-page story in the *Globe-Democrat* echoed this concern. A survey commissioned by City Bank, which bravely constructed a six-story building at 4625 Lindell in 1971 even after a much-publicized robbery at their previous 4981 West Pine location, solicited the opinions of 1,102 residents and 133 businesses. The bank president, Norman Tice, generously pledged $10,000 toward the promotion of the area. Amid comments about the need for more city services and stricter building codes, another sentiment stood out: the area's "great problem," agreed merchants and residents alike, "is crime."

"There was petty crime going on—perhaps more than petty crime," adds Will Ross, a nephrologist at Barnes-Jewish Hospital who today lives on Westmoreland Place. "There

"We are not a suburban medical school; we are an urban medical school, so we have to be part of the renovation of this area. We have to address the social ills—that's part of what we are as a medical school. We must have some role in improving the health of the community and its structure. This certainly benefits the community, but it also benefits us. Our staff lives in St. Louis, our faculty lives in St. Louis, and we want them to live close to the medical school and feel comfortable doing so. We also realize that our stature worldwide is highly dependent on how St. Louis is viewed and what we can do to uplift St. Louis.

"People come to Washington University School of Medicine because it is in the city. They really believe that our best days are ahead of us—that cities are going to be places of spontaneity, great ideas, and creativity. These are people coming in with young kids, and they want them exposed to all this culture. Our best and brightest medical students are here because they want to be in an urban enclave; this is where you study medicine. I just can't believe we would have maintained our preeminence if we were somewhere in far West County. Our place in the Central West End is one of the reasons why we are such a remarkable institution."

—Will Ross,
nephrologist and associate dean for diversity
at the Washington University School of Medicine

Hotel Ordered To Quit Brothel Operations

By E. S. EVANS
Of the Post-Dispatch Staff

Now that the Oriental Hotel has been ordered by the St. Louis Circuit Court to stop operating as a bawdy house, the city will seek similar judgments against four other midtown hotels.

Meanwhile, the Oriental's owners say they may appeal the court order handed down Friday.

Judge Michael L. Hart ordered the Oriental Hotel, 4612 Olive Street, to require identification of occupants and to give the court monthly reports of their names and lengths of stay.

The order will allow the 12-room hotel to remain open for legitimate purposes. The reports, which are to be submitted under oath, are intended to ensure that the hotel does not continue to operate as a bawdy house.

The city had sought to close all five hotels as public nuisances, as well as a sixth that has folded since the suits were filed in July 1976. The city charged that all were being regularly used for prostitution.

Miss Judith Ronzio, an assistant city counselor, said she was satisfied with Hart's ruling and would discuss it with attorneys for the other hotels.

"They may agree to court orders like this one," she stated. "If they won't, we'll have to try the suits against them."

David B. Lacks, attorney for the owners of the Oriental, said the order exceeded the judge's authority, but was uncertain whether it would be appealed to a higher court.

"No law authorizes such reports as Hart has ordered," Lacks said, "but the hotel can operate under the restrictions. Much of its business is legitimate."

The judge reported in hearings held earlier this year that 90 per cent of the Oriental's paying guests stayed for three hours or less. In 1976, room rentals ranged from none to 54 a day, Hart found, and averaged about 17 a day.

The hotel's rates are $3.75 for three hours and $8 overnight. Its operation is believed to be similar to that of the other four hotel's.

At the hearings, 14 undercover police detectives testified that on 30 occasions since last October, prostitutes on "The Stroll", a nearby area used by street-walkers, had directed them to the Oriental Hotel. There they engaged prostitutes and rooms, the policemen said.

The hotel is owned by firemen Benjamin F. Ledbetter and Matthew Miley, both assigned to the firehouse at 4810 Enright Avenue. They also operate a liquor store on the first floor of the hotel building.

The other establishments that the city sought to close after midtown residents complained of rampant prostitution in their neighborhood are the Ritz Hotel, 4049 Washington Boulevard; Alcorn Hotel, 4165 Washington; Morgan Manor Hotel, 3090 Westminster Avenue and Green Hotel, 4269 Washington. The Adams Hotel, 4295 Olive, that the city also sought to close, was condemned last winter for lack of heat.

St. Louis Post-Dispatch, **August 13, 1977**

was a bit of a 'stroll' as you walked past Maryland Plaza, and I was propositioned more than once going home. It was a challenging environment." When he visited St. Louis in 1979 to interview for medical school, Ross was walking on Kingshighway when he suddenly found himself in the middle of a gun battle as a police officer opened fire on a man just in front of him on the sidewalk.

Through the early to mid-1970s, one section of the Central West End near Washington, Walton, and Westminster was under siege because another "stroll" area had developed along Olive and Washington. In 1977, the St. Louis Circuit Court ordered the Oriental Hotel at 4612 Olive to cease operation as a "bawdy house," after residents complained of being solicited again and again by street hustlers drumming up business.

REDLINING REDUCES INFLUX OF NEW RESIDENTS

Not only were residents leaving but newcomers, attracted to urban life by a fledgling "back-to-the-city" movement, were also finding it hard to buy Central West End property. Redlining—the refusal of lending institutions to grant mortgages in areas deemed "risky"—was all too common. In 1974, a study for the Phoenix Fund confirmed that redlining was undermining real estate sales in St. Louis city. Between 1965 and 1972, home mortgage loans to city buyers by St. Louis savings and loans had decreased by more than 50 percent. And one of the areas most affected by declining mortgages, said the report, was the Central West End.

One person who was optimistic about progress in the Central West End and his own Skinker-DeBaliviere neighborhood was John G. Roach, then alderman from the Twenty-Eighth Ward and later the city's first director of the Community Development Agency, who had long worked against redlining. Although he agreed in general with the Phoenix Fund findings, he also said publicly, "Those figures end in 1974. Things have loosened up a lot, particularly in 1975. In the past few months, the savings and loans have started to come through."

Still, a 1976 study by the Association of Community Organizations for Reform Now (ACORN) provided new evidence of redlining: "There is a marked lack of mortgage activity in North St. Louis and the Central West End, and a general concentration of mortgage money in St. Louis County and beyond," said a *Post-Dispatch* article. Of the more than $468 million in mortgage loans made in St. Louis during 1975, only $2.8 million (or six-tenths of 1 per cent) went to the Central West End.

St. Louis Post-Dispatch, April 18, 1974

Alderman John G. Roach, 1975

"Filling the Urban Hole in Metropolitan Doughnut,"
St. Louis Post-DIspatch, **April 24, 1977**

Left and above, **Central West End streets, undated**

"What this shows clearly is that a massive disinvestment process is taking place, particularly by the savings and loan institutions," said Richard Ratcliff, an ACORN researcher and faculty member in sociology at Washington University. "There is far more money being collected in the city than is being put back in the form of loans. We don't think that it results from an absence of demand. We know there are hundreds of credit-worthy people out there who have been unable to get loans."

GASLIGHT SQUARE DIMS ITS LIGHTS

Meanwhile, the quirky Gaslight Square entertainment district was fading into oblivion. In 1968, an eighteen-year-old writing in to the *Post-Dispatch*'s "Ask Martha" column, worried "whether [Gaslight Square] was the place for kids our age to go for an evening of fun." No wonder the teen was asking. That May, one newspaper columnist counted twenty-two empty nightclubs and bars in the three-block district. Only twelve remained, and a fire had just destroyed the Bella Rosa and Mister D's restaurants. Laclede Gas had cut off service to a third of the hallmark gaslights because merchants had failed to pay the bills.

Crime had burgeoned, starting with the murder of a woman in the Cumberland Apartments in Gaslight Square in December 1964. Prostitutes and drug users were moving in along with "long-haired, unshaven men [who] lounge in apartment door fronts and drink beer and taunt passers-by," said a *Post-Dispatch* story. One Gaslight Square bar lost its liquor license because it allowed "immoral persons to loiter," said another article. In 1969, two students were kidnapped from a Gaslight Square coffeehouse, "The Exit," and beaten up before being dropped off in an alley behind 4400 McPherson.

Crumbling buildings in Gaslight Square, undated

The Chase Club entrance and Crazy Horse advertisement, 1979

Soon the brief, effervescent life of the district was over. "Signs telling of vacancies catch the eye. Rubble blows against the curb and across the sidewalk. Shadows move eerily beneath the darkened gas lamps. There is a feeling and an odor of decay. As a thriving center of night life and entertainment, Gaslight Square is a thing of the past," said a story. In 1972, radio station KDNA was sold, one of the last businesses in the area.

But memories lingered. In 1978, Chase Park Plaza owner Harold Koplar got into trouble with local authorities for staging a risqué act, "Le Show de Paris," which featured bare-breasted women. While police threatened to visit the hotel's Crazy Horse Saloon to make some arrests, he protested that there was "nothing vulgar, lewd or sensational about it." Further, he added, "I'm a member of the Convention Bureau and it was brought out again recently how St. Louis is very much lacking in things to do at night. Since Gaslight Square finally deteriorated and was wiped out, there hasn't been anything except some little cocktail lounges."

"353" WEIGHS IN

In 1971, developers began applying to the board of aldermen for residential project approval under the Missouri Urban Redevelopment Corporations Law known as "353" or the "blighting" law, which offered developers tax abatements and the power of eminent domain. Four parts of the Central West End qualified early as target areas: a 3.3-acre site bounded by Washington, Euclid, and just north of McPherson; a 1.9-acre site on Pershing east of DeBaliviere; a 25.6-acre site bounded by DeBaliviere on the west, Delmar on the north, Waterman on the south, and Clara on the east; and a 38-acre triangle south of Delmar and west of DeBaliviere.

Some critics opposed 353 saying that tax abatement took too much property from the tax rolls. But supporters insisted that 353 made housing redevelopment practical and affordable. "Leon Strauss of Pantheon Corp. says that tax abatement can mean a difference of $100 a month to a home buyer, and $25 to $40 a month to a renter. Buyers and renters might go elsewhere otherwise," said one 1980 newspaper story.

In 1975, the Maryland Plaza Redevelopment Corporation created by former mayor Alfonso J. Cervantes became one of those chartered under 353, which enabled Cervantes and his colleagues to acquire land and begin redevelopment

Leon Strauss (1928–1999)

Pantheon officers Carl Lehne, vice president, and Leon Strauss, president, 1977

Maryland Plaza Redevelopment Corporation, created in 1975 by Alfonso Cervantes, undated

Alfonso Cervantes (1920–1993)

Academy of the Sacred Heart, Maryland and Taylor, undated

Maryland Gardens Apartments, 4481 Maryland, 1974

efforts. Pantheon also used 353 in its rehabilitation and development efforts in the Pershing-Waterman area.

OTHER REDEVELOPMENT EFFORTS

In 1972, a 194-unit, low-rise housing complex—planned for a site bounded by Maryland, Taylor, Pershing, and St. Elizabeth Hall that was formerly the location of the Academy of the Sacred Heart–Barat Hall—received approval from the city and HUD. Called Maryland Gardens, it was the brainchild of George Hellmuth of the architectural firm Hellmuth, Obata + Kassabaum. On the health side, the Union-Sarah Realty Investment Corporation remodeled a building in the 4900 block of Delmar to serve as the Union-Sarah/Yeatman Health Center, a community health care facility.

A key generator of redevelopment activity was the Union-Sarah Economic Development Corporation (USEDC), a holding company of the nonprofit Union-Sarah Community Corporation, formed in 1967 with a $2.1 million grant from the Office of Economic Opportunity to promote economic growth in an area from Union to Sarah and Martin Luther King (then Easton) to McPherson. In 1969, the USEDC— one of only forty-two community economic development corporations across the country—won a coveted $900,000 federal grant to help low-income residents start their own businesses. It worked with Commerce Bank and the federal government on a $1.2 million redevelopment of the historic Sherwood Court Apartments, built to house diplomats attending the World's Fair, at North Taylor and McPherson Avenues.

"The USEDC was created out of Lyndon Johnson's War on Poverty. I served on the board from 1967 to 1973, when I had to resign to be in the governor's office. They made some real estate investments, but they were not successful in regenerating the neighborhood," said Charles Valier, who was then a state representative from the area. "They just didn't have the scale, and it wasn't the force that it was intended to be."

Amid a welter of projects, the federal Community Services Administration gave the group a two-year, $1.5 million grant in 1976, while warning them that they had to develop a closer relationship with city planning officials or risk losing future funds. The USEDC continued to move forward, proposing a $4.5 million renovation project for the General Van and Storage Co. at 4908 Delmar and, in 1978, the conversion of the Roosevelt Hotel at Euclid and Delmar into an apartment building.

The newly restored Sherwood Court Apartments, *St. Louis Post-Dispatch,* June 23, 1977

"In 1969, I could have bought a house on Fullerton's Westminster Place for $10,000—*seriously*, $10,000. Instead, I bought a house on Westmoreland Place in 1975 for $60,000. I grew up in the city so I was willing to stay; most of my friends left. When I was police commissioner from 1981 to 1985, crime on Westmoreland was bad, mostly crimes against property. In that period, the block where the Chase Park Plaza is located was the highest crime area in the city for crimes against property. Anyone who parked across from the Chase had a 50 percent chance of his or her car being broken into or stolen.

"At my house, a man broke in, and then he came back and tried to break in again, but that time I was home and we caught him. He was a young man, higher than a kite, and he didn't know where he was or what he was doing. I confronted him, and I was scared to death. It was harrowing. He was charged with more than forty robberies in my neighborhood—all to raise money for his drugs."

—Charles Valier,
attorney and former Missouri state representative,
counsel to the Missouri governor,
and police commissioner for the city of St. Louis

Left, people dining in the Central West End, 1962. *Right,* Miller Newton (left), executive director of the Mid-City Community Congress with (from left) the Rev. Paul Harting, St. Louis Catholic Cathedral; Rev. Robert W. Wilden, Second Presbyterian Church; James H. Wollbrinck, a lawyer, and Rev. Andrew Kunz, Trinity Espiscopal Church, *St. Louis Post-Dispatch,* July 13, 1966

SOME BRIGHT SPOTS

While all this was going on, residents were making valiant attempts at change. A new citizens' group, the Mid-City Community Congress, with a storefront office at 4007 Delmar, formed to promote civic improvement and address racial inequities in a 300-block area covering "Gaslight Square, many of the city's best hotels, the private streets off Kingshighway, where Mayor A. J. Cervantes and other community leaders live, and long stretches of desolate slums inhabited by low-income Negro families," said a 1968 *Post-Dispatch* account. A host of prominent St. Louisans supported the effort, including architect Gyo Obata, McDonnell Douglas chairman James S. McDonnell, and Episcopal bishop George Cadigan. "We can do one of two things," said physician and area resident John Grant. "We can build a wall around us to protect us in our private streets or we can go out and become concerned about the larger area around us."

In 1970, the *Globe-Democrat* featured a 600-member group called "Women for City Living," which had been working actively toward neighborhood improvement in concert with police and city officials. Formed in 1969, this organization—which included its president Delphine McClellan, Linda Eyerman, Virginia Feinberg, Anna Busch,

Ida McClain, and later president Joyce Littlefield—focused on enforcing building codes and zoning ordinances, halting prostitution, ridding the area of derelict autos and rats, helping young families move in, tracking down absentee landlords, and then prodding them to keep up their buildings.

Then McClellan, a lifelong area resident who lived at 5757 Lindell, moved on to broader efforts. At the request of Mayor Cervantes, she became co-chair of an effort called the Women's Crusade against Crime, a city-wide program to fight crime, force the demolition of rundown buildings, improve zoning, and urge high school dropouts to return to school. In her 2011 obituary, McClellan was described as "the arch mother of citizen anti-crime efforts in St. Louis."

Another neighborhood group, TW3, formed in the early 1970s to combat such "rooms-by-the-hour" hotels as the Oriental and to urge the city to create a park at Olive and Walton. The group, headed by Art Perry, represented several blocks in that area: 4500–4700 Westminster, 4700–4800 Washington, and 500–600 Walton, plus Trinity Episcopal and Second Presbyterian Churches. They found strong support for their work from the energetic, dedicated Mary Stolar, who served from 1973 to 1981 as Twenty-Fifth Ward alderman, succeeding her husband, Henry.

The Women's Crusade against Crime, 1970

Women for City Living, 1972

"I came to the Central West End in 1954 to work for Kean Drug at Euclid and Laclede, and then I left the store in 1981. I stayed in my home on Westminster, which we had bought in 1966, while working and traveling for Eli Lilly.

"What was it like for people of color in the earlier years? The merchants were not serving blacks in the front ends of restaurants, cafés, and bars; there was a back entrance for the service personnel and the people who worked in the ABC apartments, the Ellington, Pierre Chouteau, and others. They all had black service people or day workers. They were not served in those retail establishments then. Working in the drugstore, I was the one giving service so I refused to go in the back doors. There was not hostility, but we were all supposed to know our place.

"One reason I stayed was Forest Park: going there with Henry and Mary Stolar and others. It was like a giant source of energy; you went there to read, enjoy nature, meet others; run, bicycle, have a meal, take your kids for a picnic. I also remember walking home from the drugstore during the 1970s, and I'd stop, have a drink, and dance in Herbie's. I knew all the folks there, gay and straight. I was the 'drug pusher' for all of them, so I was well known. Sometimes I'd have my wife meet me there, and it was great fun."

—Art Perry,
Central West End resident, pharmacist, and activist

A Joint Board—originally composed of Westminster Presbyterian, Union Avenue Christian, and Pilgrim Congregational Churches and later of First Unitarian, Second Presbyterian, and Trinity Episcopal—formed to examine neighborhood needs and find ways to deal with unemployment, provide health services, and fight for adequate housing. They were sponsors of a Neighborhood Youth Corps, plus tutoring through the Westminster Neighborhood School and other programs for children, and in 1972 they mounted the first in a series of Mustard Seed Festivals to raise funds for their youth-related projects.

A new program developed on Euclid: the United Black Teen Center, run by Jesse Todd, program director for the Union-Sarah Economic Development Corporation. Union-Sarah provided workers to rehab the building, while businessmen in the area took care of the rent. In this center, Todd held rap sessions about responsibility, while also providing space for recreation; he helped young men find jobs. "It's a tough new day," said Todd in 1972. "No more games. It's time to dig in, stay and deal with the problems." Thanks to a $250,000 grant from the Danforth Foundation, another new program—the Learning Center, located in the former Wednesday Club building at Taylor and Westminster—opened to provide programs for teachers.

The United Black Teen Center on Euclid run by Jesse Todd, program director for the Union-Sarah Economic Development Corporation, 1972

Jesse Todd, *St. Louis Post-Dispatch*, June 6, 1972

FOUR CENTRAL WEST END HEROES

C. Perry Bascom (1936–2014) A longtime resident of Pershing Place and lawyer with Bryan Cave, Bascom was appointed by Mayor Cervantes to be a judge of the Housing Court in 1970. A member of Trinity Episcopal Church, he sent his children to New City School and served on its board. In a 1970 newspaper article, he said, "I think there is a style of living in the city you can't find elsewhere."

Mary Stolar (1940–1987) She ran for alderman of the Twenty-Fifth Ward in 1972 just after her husband, Henry, stepped down—and won twice, serving from 1973 to 1981. During that time, she battled tirelessly for the Central West End, sponsoring the historic district legislation and bills to promote the area's redevelopment. Later, Mayor Vincent Schoemehl named her head of Forest Park Forever, and she served energetically in that role until her early death.

Renni Shuter (1937–2015) She was active in real estate for forty years, specializing in the Central West End. She was also a part owner of the *West End Word*, writing a column called "Candlelight and Crumbs." Elected to the St. Louis school board, she helped found a magnet school. At the First Unitarian Church, she established a fund to promote social welfare programs in the Central West End.

William Chapman (1924–1998) Rector of Trinity Episcopal Church from 1970 to 1993, he was committed to social justice. Amid the AIDS crisis of the 1980s, his church ministered to many people with the disease. He also fought racial inequality. He was a leader of the Interfaith Partnership, the Joint Community Board, and the Central West End Association, as well as a board member of the Union-Sarah Economic Development Corporation.

Ad in *St. Louis Post-Dispatch*, May 3, 1970

Left, **William Fellenz at the entrance to his antique shop, 439 North Euclid, 1969**

By 1972, new businesses had come to life in the commercial district. "From Barney's Soul Food Restaurant on Delmar to a car wash on Forest Park Parkway, the scene shifts dramatically," said one article. "At McPherson Avenue, antique shops—refugees from Gaslight Square—coexist with 'head shops' and clothing stores catering to the young." One of the best-known "refugee" antique shops, owned by William Fellenz, was located in a building at 439 North Euclid that had formerly housed carriages and later electric cars. A local clothing store was the Gypsy Cowboy, owned by longtime resident Herbert Balaban, who also opened the popular Café Balaban in 1972 and then sold it in 1986. Another restaurant, Culpepper's, was opened by Herb Glazer and Mary McCabe in 1977.

Among the new restaurants, one of the earliest and longest-lasting was Duff's, which opened in 1972. It was the whimsical, shoestring effort of Karen Duffy and her first husband, Dan Duffy, which began in a vacant Euclid storefront with a waitstaff of four and an eighteen-year-old chef. A *West End Word* review described it as having a purple ceiling and "a marvelous conglomeration of art, ranging from campy to nice." The restaurant was successful and later expanded to the south. It also became known for hosting readings with its neighbor, Left Bank Books.

"In our minds the restaurant would be part of a neighborhood, where people would come to meet and eat. It wouldn't be expensive, but it would be high-quality food, not fast food. We started by knocking plaster off the walls, painting, refinishing the floors. People would come along and say: 'What are you guys doing in there? Need any help?' And they would come in and help us refinish a chair. I like to say it was magic. It all came together.

"Balaban's opened in April 1972, and Duff's in July, so we were the pioneer restaurants. Debbie, the witch, was next door. Frank Marmino had Europa 390, and next to him was a movie theater. Pete Rothschild was to the north. There were a lot of antique stores that had been in Gaslight Square. It felt like we were part of a neighborhood that included gay, straight, black, white, young, old. So that was exciting. And there was a willingness to work for nothing. Nobody was making any money, but we were having a very good time."

—Karen Duffy,
former owner of Duff's Restaurant

New City School, "a recent addition to the private schools in the Central West End," said the *St. Louis Post-Dispatch*, March 5, 1972

Other restaurants coming to the area included the Art Deco–style Griffin's Plaza at 1 Maryland Plaza.

Some new businesses also began moving into Maryland Plaza. By 1974, the mayor's son, Alfonso Cervantes Jr.—who, like his father, lived in the area—had opened the Maryland Avenue Screening Room, a restaurant–movie theater. In 1977, the Davidson Gallery was selling antique craftwork including folk-art-style quilts and weather vanes; on Euclid, Tricia Woo's had Missouri craft items, including rugs, baskets, and contemporary quilts. Inglis Ltd. advertised such antiques as a mahogany library table and pine hutch. By 1979, the Kamp Gallery, Plaza Consignment Gallery, Hirschfeld Gallery, and Surprise! all lined Maryland Plaza, while nearby was the Martin Schweig Gallery at 4657 Maryland.

FOUNDING OF NEW CITY SCHOOL AND OTHERS

Another major step forward came as Central West End parents scrambled for schools to fill the void left by the closing of Barat Hall and City House. In 1969, a group headed by later Washington University Law School dean Tad Foote organized the New City School, originally with ninety-five elementary students, in quarters leased from the First Unitarian Church at Waterman and Kingshighway. In 1971, the

"By the time I arrived in 1981, New City School had about 245 kids, and it was a place of joyful learning, a diverse setting where kids could grow and learn. I viewed this as an opportunity to bring some theories to life and work with some exceptionally talented people.

"The neighborhood was spotty at best. There were wonderful houses, still filled with grandeur and lots of charisma, next to a house that might be boarded up, next to a house that clearly was in a state of disrepair. The area on Waterman between Lake and Kingshighway had quite a few boarded-up homes. Walking on the street would always be a question.

There was lots of potential, lots of really good people, but an area that had been underinvested for quite some time.

"Schools are really about hope—the hope we have for our children and their future. Without a school in a neighborhood, it is questionable whether families are going to buy there or remain there. What New City School did was say to everybody: You can live in the Central West End. There is going to be a wonderful school within walking distance. The presence of a school that by design was inclusive, where kids really wanted to learn, stabilized the neighborhood."

—Thomas Hoerr,
emeritus head of New City School

Reflection

Sixth-grader Melinda Baber engages in a discussion with her Crossroads School classmates, 1980.

Students at Crossroads School watch election results come in, 1980.

school—which then had 150 students and a growing staff—moved into the old Mary Institute building at Lake Avenue and Waterman and spent $40,000 to renovate the space. The school was fully accredited in 1977, and four years later hired its longtime, much-loved director, Thomas Hoerr.

Two other schools also got under way. A different group started the Westminster School in Second Presbyterian, at first with fourteen fifth- and sixth-graders and eventually with students from kindergarten through sixth grade. But financial problems ensued, and it closed in the mid-1970s, sending many of its students to New City. In 1974, Carol and Arthur Lieber founded Crossroads School (now Crossroads College Preparatory School) for junior high students in four rooms of a community center in the Laclede Town area, but it moved in 1976 to 4532 Lindell and then in 1980 to 500 DeBaliviere. In 1979, it advertised tongue-in-cheek for a math teacher willing to work "for respectably low wages."

Public schools also changed as magnet schools came into being in 1976. The Stix School at 226 South Euclid metamorphosed into the Investigative Learning Center and soon expanded to 425 students. A Business and Office Magnet High School opened in the old Temple Israel Education Building at 5017 Washington, though it soon relocated downtown, and the alternative Metro High School took its place.

HISTORIC DISTRICTS FORM

During this period, there were three building-related victories: for a single house, for a district, and for the entire Central West End. In 1973, first Henry and then Mary Stolar, not only aldermen but also Kingsbury Place residents, began prodding the city on behalf of their neighbors to create a new Kingsbury Place–Washington Terrace historic district. Adding urgency to this cause was a curious situation. Louise Woodruff Johnston, a seventy-two-year-old widow who had lived for most of her life at 4 Kingsbury Place, had died, and her will called for the demolition of her Mediterranean-style home. Shocked, her Kingsbury neighbors filed suit against the executor of her estate, Mercantile Trust Co. If they could create a historic district, demolitions of this kind would be prohibited in the future.

In 1973, a circuit court ruled in favor of the executors, but neighbors persisted in their attempts to block demolition. Then nearly a year later, after the historic district ordinance had passed, Mercantile filed a suit contending that Kingsbury Place and Washington Terrace have "no historical significance not shared by many areas." But in April 1975, the Missouri Court of Appeals ruled in a 2-to-1 decision against "senseless" demolition, saying, "the public interest in maintaining good housing in the city of St. Louis took a

Kingsbury Place home of Louise Woodruff Johnston, at risk of being torn down, 1973

Louise Woodruff Johnston, c. 1901–1973

MR. AND MRS. RICHARD McCULLOCH, 4394 Westminster place, as they sailed Nov 8 on the Ile de France for a six weeks' tour of Europe. —Ella Barnett, New York

Richard and Mary Grace McCulloch of 4394 Westminster, about to embark on a six-week tour of Europe, 1929

higher priority over [the] provision in Mrs. Johnston's will." When the Missouri Supreme Court refused to review this decision, the house was safe.

As one story pointed out, this wasn't the first time a Central West End resident had decided to have her home torn down after her death. Mary Grace McCulloch lived at 4394 Westminster Place after her marriage to Richard McCulloch, president of the United Railways Co. and St. Louis Car Co., who died in 1940. She was also the daughter of John Beggs, a utilities tycoon who left an estate of $54 million. But she loudly insisted that she didn't want any family except the McCullochs ever to occupy her cherished, eighteen-room mansion—so after she died in 1956, the house came down.

In 1974, the City Plan Commission recommended creating a Central West End historic district, bounded by DeBaliviere and Boyle, Lindell and Delmar. As the board of aldermen considered the measure, Joseph W. B. Clark, director of public safety, worried that this district would pose bureaucratic impediments to development. Joyce Littlefield, a member of the commission, wondered whether it might place financial burdens on less-well-off residents trying to keep up their properties. But supporters felt that "historic district designation is viewed as protection against unwarranted demolition and against new construction and repairs judged to deter from the quality of a given neighborhood," reported the *Post-Dispatch*. Alderman Mary Stolar introduced the bill; C. B. Broussard from the Twenty-Sixth Ward and Samuel Kennedy from the Nineteenth Ward were also sponsors. The Landmarks Association offered key support and also worked to place buildings on the National Register of Historic Places.

That June, the bill passed the board of aldermen by a 25–2 vote, and Mayor John H. Poelker signed it into law. As the measure said, this new "Central West End Historic District has architectural and historical value which should be preserved for the people of the City of St. Louis and the State of Missouri." Further, the preservation of buildings and parks would "serve as a visible reminder of the historic, architectural and cultural heritage of the City." As time went on, the measure would also have a practical effect: giving developers access to investment tax credits and federal or state historic tax credits, which could substantially lower the cost of renovating buildings. The Central West End became the third historic district in the city, along with Lafayette Square and Kingsbury Place–Washington Terrace.

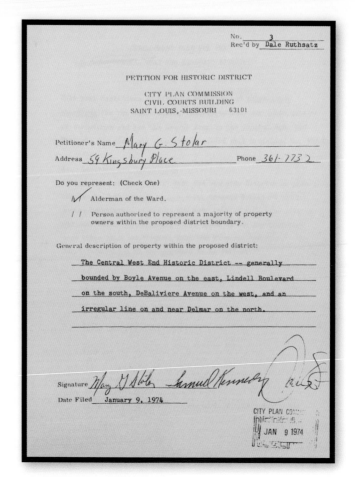

The petition for the Central West End Historic District, filed by Mary Stolar, 1974

St. Louis Post-Dispatch, **March 18, 1974**

INAPPROPRIATE INFILL?

In 1970, the St. Louis Housing Authority announced that it would build a 397-unit apartment building for low-income seniors at 4451 Forest Park Boulevard, though newspapers called it "a cause of controversy and conflict." Some Central West End residents opposed the $7.4 million project because they thought there were too many federally financed low-income developments in the area. Already, a 128-unit project stood at West Pine and Taylor, while another 147-unit had gone up at 5655 Kingsbury Avenue. Further, a new drug treatment center had opened at Pershing and DeBaliviere.

So in 1971, Women for City Living hosted a public meeting at the Cathedral School to air public opinion—most of it opposed to the thirteen-story building, which many also saw as vastly oversized and too densely occupied for the site. Afterward, Joyce Littlefield on behalf of the Women for City Living group and Ida McClain for the Waterman Community Association filed suit to block its construction. They hadn't opposed the first two senior-citizen buildings nor the drug center, said one of their members, and they certainly weren't against the project on racial grounds. While they were happy to take their share of urban responsibility, they saw this project as one too many.

Housing For Elderly Here Approved

By a Washington Correspondent of the Post-Dispatch

WASHINGTON, March 31 — The Department of Housing and Urban Development has approved the funding for a $7,400,000 apartment building for the elderly in St. Louis.

The project, to be constructed at 4451 Forest Park Boulevard, will be a 13-story building to include 300 efficiency apartments and 97 one-bedroom units, all for rental to older persons with limited incomes.

HUD will provide $7,396,881 to the Housing Authority of St. Louis, which, in turn, will contract with the Parkview Apartments Housing Development to build the apartments.

The Parkview firm is a joint venture of Ira H., Melvin and L. W. Dubinsky and Clarence B. and William H. Deal of St. Louis.

A spokesman for the St. Louis Housing Authority said construction should begin within the next few weeks and should be finished by the end of next year. A hearing for residents of the area was to be held today at City Hall.

Apartments will be available to men 65 years old or older and women 62 or older, or younger persons who are physically disabled. Rentals will be at standard public housing rates, based on the incomes of the tenants.

Approval of the contract was announced by Senators Stuart Symington and Thomas F. Eagleton, Missouri Democrats.

Rosalynn Carter, wife of Democratic presidential candidate Jimmy Carter, says she plans to be highly influential in the White House, especially in two areas where she has special interest — mental health and programs for the elderly.

Mrs. Carter made her remarks today at the Chase-Park Plaza Hotel in her first visit to St. Louis. She met with reporters before visiting the Parkview apartments, a residence for the elderly, at 4451 Forest Park Boulevard.

A thirteen-story building for low-income seniors was approved at 4451 Forest Park Blvd., despite protests by Women for City Living, 1971.

The first issue of a brand-new neighborhood newspaper, the *West End Word*, was published in August 1972 to "challenge old ideas . . . and, hopefully, provoke the growth of new ones," said the first editorial.

But Thomas Costello, director of the St. Louis Housing Authority, insisted in 1971 that "we have the legal authority to go ahead on the Forest Park project, and we're going to go ahead"—though he added that he knew this decision was unpopular and he was glad that he didn't have political ambitions himself. A judge dismissed the two suits, as well as an appeal. Even the *Post-Dispatch* threw its support to the plan, saying "the construction of this project does not spell an end to the West End. Those who continue to associate this particular development with the decline of the area are probably doing more damage than could possibly be done by a few hundred senior citizens with a decent place to live on Forest Park." The building was finished in the spring of 1972.

THE *WEST END WORD*— "UNASHAMED BOOSTERS"

A large section of the Central West End—from Boyle to Kingshighway and from Olive to Lindell—already had a chatty newsletter, *Near By*, headquartered at 459 North Boyle. On its masthead, the paper said that it was "published in and for this neighborhood, its self-awareness and future design." In one 1959 issue, it printed an article asking people to send baby teeth to the Baby Teeth Survey, 4484 West Pine, where they would be tested for strontium-90 they might have absorbed from 1948–1953 nuclear testing. Another column, "New Moves," chronicled the arrival of new homeowners, such as physicians Sumner Holtz to 4537 Pershing and Hugh Foster to 5 Lenox Place. "The old

Three *West End Word* pioneers—Robert Duffy, Renni Shuter, and Ellie Chapman—in front of Duff's Restaurant

Perry Chrysler house has been sold to a trio of gentlemen . . . William E. Follin, S.E. Hall and Maxwell Moulton [who] . . . feel apartments are a waste of money in that the end results are not ownership but cancelled checks."

One day in 1972, four talented, energetic members of Trinity Episcopal Church gathered in the Kingsbury Place backyard of Linda Eyerman (now Sun Smith-Foret) to talk about the neighborhood. "Somebody said, 'Why don't we start a newspaper?' It sounded like a good thing to do, and we figured we could probably scare up $100 apiece to get it going. We would sell ads to pay for the printing. And we did that," recalls Ellie Chapman, one of the four founders along with Eyerman, Jack Lowell, and Robert Duffy. Early on, Lowell moved out of town but Suzanne Goell, Mary Bartley, Margaret Grant, and Renni Shuter came on board.

"In the first issue, I wrote an editorial on the front page," recalls Duffy, which said that "'Frankly, we're unashamed boosters. We want this neighborhood not only to thrive in the moment but also to survive into the future. It's too good to waste.' It was great fun, but it was serious fun. We had a mission. It was all done on various dining room tables—and off it went." What was that mission? "Thus comes the *West End Word*," said that first editorial, "—straightforwardly, honestly, sometimes irreverently—with a desire to serve and entertain this unique and valuable sliver of the earth."

Reflection

"We bought a three-story house in the Central West End, which cost $15,000. It was a great house and a great street: there were people who had lived there for many years but also these feisty kids moving in, feeling like this was a new frontier. There was a sense of connection between us, that we all shared a commitment to the city and to the neighborhood.

"But as time went along, there were divisions. At one point, the fear of people walking through was rather critical and some wanted to dig a moat around our block, so there was a lot of putting up of fences and closing off of little walkways that used to connect the streets. But in general there was a feeling that we wanted to preserve what we had without being too exclusionary about it.

"It was an exciting time to be involved in community affairs, because no matter what our politics were, we all shared a notion that this was something worth saving, not just the Central West End, but the whole city of St. Louis."

—Robert Duffy,
cofounder, *West End Word*;
former features editor, *St. Louis Post-Dispatch*

A helicopter heading to St. Louis Children's Hospital, 1970

Right away, the newspaper caught on, recalls Ellie Chapman. "Everybody wanted to write a story; everybody had something to say. One of our biggest problems was how to get it to people, because we all wanted to be in on writing or thinking up stories; nobody wanted to be in on the picking up from the printer and putting them in people's front yards. But I think people really appreciated getting this funny-looking little newspaper on their doorsteps."

While they often tackled the fate of individual buildings, adds Duffy, at times their lens would widen to broader issues. "When Children's Hospital proposed building across Kingshighway and taking over some parkland, there was a huge uproar. No one wanted intrusion like that into the park—or to block one of the great urban vistas in the city—so the *West End Word* took a position and a lot of people got involved." In 1978, with Forest Park under siege from encroaching parking lots, institutional expansion, and golf courses, the *Word* begged for the development of a master plan.

Eventually, Suzanne Goell became the newspaper's longtime editor and then owner. In his introduction to the book *The Days and Nights of the Central West End*, Virginia Publishing Co.'s Jeffrey Fister lauded her, saying, "if Smith-Foret was the spark [that started the newspaper], Goell was . . . the glue." She was followed as owner in 1986 by Ellen Cusumano and Steve Trampe, then in 1989 by Jeffrey Fister, who had also founded Virginia Publishing Corp. in 1972.

THE SAM WAH LAUNDRY AFFAIR

In her book *The Days and Nights of the Central West End*, Suzanne Goell told the story of two Chinese brothers, Gee One and Gee Hong, who had lived and worked at 4381 Laclede for fifty-six years, operating the small Sam Wah Laundry.

"The Gee brothers washed and hand-ironed shirts for a quarter," she wrote. "The tickets were written in Chinese, and the indelible initials they marked inside shirt collars seemed to have nothing to do with the owners, but they always knew whose laundry was whose. Their customers were very loyal." But in 1979, their building was condemned because it didn't comply with the building code. "Gee Hong and Gee One were ordered evicted if repairs were not made."

So a group of friends, headed by Becky Glenn and E. F. Porter Jr., got together to help. The Washington University Medical Center Redevelopment Corporation donated $2,000 and Rosati-Kain students made "Save Sam Wah" buttons. Altogether, the campaign raised enough to fix the building, and they arranged with the landlord to let the Gee brothers live there until they died. "As soon as the last brother died, the building was torn down and made into a parking lot," wrote Goell.

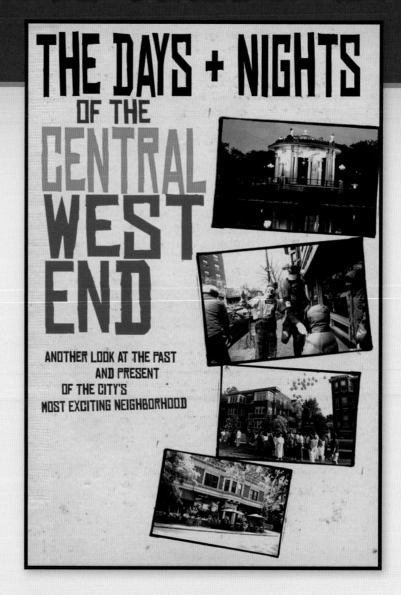

THE DAYS + NIGHTS OF THE CENTRAL WEST END

ANOTHER LOOK AT THE PAST AND PRESENT OF THE CITY'S MOST EXCITING NEIGHBORHOOD

Vignette

In the 1970s, former mayor Alfonso J. Cervantes worked with Harold Koplar and Joyce Littlefield on a controversial plan for Maryland Plaza revitalization.

KOPLAR AND CERVANTES TEAM UP

In 1975, Maryland Plaza became eligible for a property tax break under the Missouri Redevelopment Law, and "former Mayor Alfonso J. Cervantes plans to submit a redevelopment plan for that area," said news accounts. Cervantes, mayor from 1965 to 1973, was determined to do something about the plaza's deterioration, so he formed a consortium that included his ally Chase Park Plaza owner Harold Koplar, with Joyce Littlefield (later replaced by June Gooch) as redevelopment director. He set up his own office on the second floor of the Medical Arts Building, renamed the Maryland Plaza Building.

Even before the 353 designation, Cervantes and Koplar had formed the Maryland Plaza Redevelopment Corporation and consulted with Hellmuth, Obata + Kassabaum principal George Hellmuth, who had grown up on Maryland. He came up with an outsized and controversial plan, which included a fountain and ornate lights. But the strangest piece of all called for paving part of the street with cobblestones so that cars would be forced to slow down and drivers would notice items in the store windows. The *West End Word* dubbed these cobblestones and other odd parts of the plan its "Disneyland" aspects. "We hope that changes will be kept within the subdued style of the area, without stage-set overtones," it added.

Maryland Plaza fountain reconstruction, undated

In 1976, a $1 million loan from the Missouri Housing Development Commission kicked off the new $11 million redevelopment. Pantheon was in charge of the construction, which would begin with the renovation of the Fairmont Hotel, now owned by Cervantes. While the Fairmont project was a success, some residents fought a proposed rezoning so that seven Victorian-style homes on the north side of Maryland Plaza could be transformed from residences into shops. In 1974, one group filed to block the project; then in 1976, three Central West End residents—Martin Schweig Jr., James Dwyer Jr., and George Schlapp—also filed a lawsuit saying that the plans would pose "a serious threat to the continued stability of one of the city's outstanding neighborhoods." But this suit was dismissed.

As time went on, the *West End Word* also opposed the transformation of the houses. "It seems foolish to incur lawsuits and other difficulties in order to change homes to commercial property in an area where the market in residential property is currently booming, while commercial space goes begging," they said in 1975. "The unique quality of our area is due to the superior residential areas surrounding the Plaza."

In the end, some of the houses were converted to commercial space, and a string of largely unsuccessful businesses moved in: the Victorian Club, Slay's, Froebe's wine bar with a waterfall in the corner. In the old Saks building, a Koplar venture—ParaFunAlley, intended to be a thirty-store complex, which included such stores as Alice's and Heffalumps—came in and soon left. In 1981, Cervantes tried to build a large garage in the area, but neighborhood opposition prevailed.

REDLINING SPAWNS THE CENTRAL WEST END SAVINGS AND LOAN

A new savings and loan opened in 1979 at 401 DeBaliviere, with the offices of Pantheon Corp., a firm specializing in rehabilitation of older buildings, on the second floor.

After the passage of a federal disclosure law in 1975, St. Louis adopted an ordinance aimed at preventing redlining. Any bank receiving city funds would have to post a sign saying that it was not engaged in this practice. It would also have to provide the Community Development Agency with records of lending practices.

But a new savings institution was under development that would combat redlining practices. A group of ten residents organized the Central West End Savings and Loan Association and sought approvals for a state charter, which was granted in 1977. The goal of the association, said incorporator Kathleen Hamilton, was to be a "grassroots financial institution." Hamilton also testified before the US Senate's Committee on Banking, Housing, and Urban Affairs, chaired by Senator William Proxmire, in support of a bill, the Community Reinvestment Act, that would bar lenders from redlining in urban areas. The measure passed in 1977, and in 1978 a House panel voted in favor of an anti-redlining measure.

In September 1979, this new association finally celebrated its grand opening in the old Dorr and Zeller building at 401 DeBaliviere, after a long battle with New Age Federal Savings

"[Realtors] felt it was their sacred duty to tell us that if we chose to live in the west end, I would be assaulted promptly, our house would be burglarized, and our as yet unborn children could not safely walk the streets. The lectures universally ended on the upbeat: they always knew of the most darling townhouses in Creve Coeur, just the sort of thing a nice young couple like us would love. . . . This performance was given many, many times, with only the most minute changes."

—Excerpt from the *West End Word*, December 1972
"Undersell in the Central West End"
by Anna Navarro

Force For Rebirth

We read with great interest the recent articles on the status of current redevelopment in the city, and wish to congratulate the *Post-Dispatch* and Kevin Horrigan and Patricia Degener on their clarity and objectivity.

As the anchor tenant on DeBaliviere, we at Central West End Savings and Loan can see revitalization occurring around us on a daily basis. We are one of the first, urban, neighborhood-originated new savings institutions in the United States, and the first new savings and loan in the St. Louis area in 25 years. We were chartered to make possible a lending institution dedicated to being a strong force in the rebirth of the city.

The *Post-Dispatch* should be commended on such an informative series which clearly shows the positive potential and future growth of city life.

Kathleen O'C. Hamilton
Vice President-Marketing

St. Louis Post-Dispatch, July 19, 1980

and Loan Association at 1401 North Kingshighway, which was worried about competition. They were "the first new savings and loan association in the St. Louis area in a quarter century," said a *Post-Dispatch* account. One incorporator, Thomas Scatizzi, was managing officer; Hamilton, Jean Vieth, and Jewel Hunter were vice presidents; and Jesse Horstman was chairman. The other five incorporators—Gary Werths, George Murray, David P. Allen, Fred Couts, and Wade Granberry—were directors. At the time of the dedication, deposits had already reached $2 million, and they had 1,000 accounts. Two years later, those totals had grown to more than $4 million and 2,500 accounts.

Insurance redlining was also a problem, when companies refused to write or renew insurance policies for city residents. Another sticking point was insurers' insistence upon charging rates based on the replacement cost of the house rather than its market value. By 1979, several major insurance companies—faced with pressure from homeowners and advocacy groups—began backing away from these policies.

Skinker-Debaliviere Decline: These three photos from the *West End Word* show the deterioration in the neighborhood during the 1960s and 1970s.

PANTHEON AND OTHER EFFORTS AT IMPROVEMENT

Upstairs from the Central West End Savings and Loan Association in the Dorr and Zeller building were the offices of Pantheon Corp., a construction firm specializing in redevelopment efforts. Before moving to DeBaliviere, the company—founded in 1972 to focus on urban construction—was headquartered in a former casket showroom on Laclede Avenue. The owner of Pantheon was Leon Strauss, whom Suzanne Goell

described in *The Days and Nights of the Central West End*. "The first thing you notice about Leon Strauss is his smile—big, warm, and quite engaging," she wrote. "He looks as if he would be most comfortable with his sleeves rolled up for work."

"In the late 1960s, Leon was first to go in and renovate a lot of the run-down apartment buildings on Pershing and Waterman, and he did it on a large scale using private money and city tax abatements," said Charles Valier. "In the USEDC, we dabbled in real estate, but it was peanuts—not significant enough to have a major impact. But Leon rehabbed those apartments, made them livable units, and brought in families who weren't selling drugs. The change was palpable, it really was. I give Leon a lot of credit for turning things around. Outside of the efforts by Washington University, he was the hero."

In 1975, newspapers were talking about Strauss's dramatic makeover of "the seedy Convent Gardens building, near the St. Louis Cathedral and directly on the edge of the West End's private-street area, [which] had a transient population and was often visited by the police." Strauss, along with his partner Donn Lipton of Lipton Realty, had "played the role of rescuing angel in an area that was precariously balanced between renewal and decay." After buying the seven-story brick building at 4497 Pershing for only $65,000, Strauss reconfigured it, whittling down the number of units from 102 efficiencies to 83 apartments, including one- and two-bedroom units. "The city is fighting for its life," said Strauss, and "we need fighters."

After Strauss converted the Fairmont Hotel from a 100-room hotel to a 63-unit apartment building, he undertook an even more sweeping effort in 1976, when he began collecting property for a $28 million redevelopment in a 48-acre site just west of the Central West End around

A typical unit in the rehabbed Convent Gardens Apartments, 1975

St Louis Post-Dispatch, January 26, 1975

Leon Strauss (*left*) of Pantheon Corp. and Donn Lipton (*second from left*) of Lipton Realty received 1975 Homer Awards for their work on Convent Gardens.

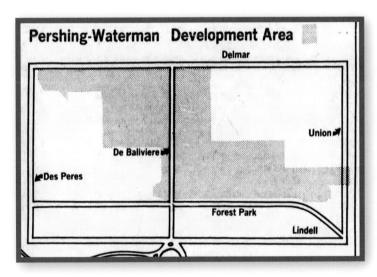

Map showing Pershing-Waterman redevelopment area, 1977

Pershing and Waterman. There he planned to rehabilitate 864 apartments and build 358 others on vacant lots over a ten-year period, with backing in large part from Mercantile Trust Co., headed by city booster Don Lasater. Supporting the project was then Twenty-Eighth Ward alderman and later mayor Vincent Schoemehl Jr., Twenty-Fifth Ward alderman Mary Stolar, and the Skinker-DeBaliviere Community Council, headed by Calvin Stuart. Strauss himself bought a home in the Central West End on Washington Terrace.

His firm started work in 1977 on the first of the eighty-five buildings they would tackle, a three-story apartment building at 5535 Waterman. During the first year, their goal was to fix up some eighteen apartments within that building, each around 1,500 square feet in size. By then, the scope of the project had grown to creating around 1,800 housing units over 115 acres and spending some $60 million. A new addition to the staff was John Roach, who had resigned as Community Development Agency director to become Strauss's executive director of the Pershing-Waterman project. In the first seven weeks after its initial Waterman units came on the market, the company sold seventeen out of eighteen available.

WASHINGTON UNIVERSITY STEPS IN

The Washington University School of Medicine and its surrounding hospitals were well aware that their neighborhood to the north was in trouble. "People don't realize when you go to the Central West End now what it was like in the 1970s," said radiologist Ronald Evens. "It was seedy. It was dirty. It was high crime. It was prostitutes. It was people drunk on the streets. So the issue became, 'Oh, my God, what are we going to do about that?'"

And crime wasn't confined to the neighborhood. It spread to the parking lots, even the corridors, of the hospitals. Through the 1970s, the Barnes and Jewish Hospital publications were filled with stories about how to foil purse-snatchers or navigate parking lots safely. As late as 1983, said the *Globe-Democrat*, three men robbed the Barnes Hospital cafeteria; physician Leonard Tolmach gave chase onto Kingshighway, where the men fired two shots at the doctor before vanishing into Forest Park.

Already in 1962, several institutions—Jewish, Barnes, Children's, and Barnard Hospitals; the Washington University School of Medicine; and the Central Institute for the Deaf—had formed an alliance called the Washington University School of Medicine and Associated Hospitals (WUMSAH), later renamed the Washington University Medical Center.

Land clearance began along Forest Park Avenue to make way for the Blue Cross campus, 1975.

This busy Central West End street was part of the redevelopment area, 1975.

William Danforth, vice chancellor for medical affairs, speaking at a groundbreaking ceremony for McDonnell Hall, 1967. Seated at the far right is Chancellor Thomas Eliot.

Construction in progress on McDonnell Hall, 1968

An affiliation between Jewish Hospital and Washington University followed in 1963. The new president of WUMSAH in 1965 was medical school cardiologist William Danforth, also recently named vice chancellor for medical affairs at the School of Medicine.

At that point, the medical complex had a major stake in the Central West End, with its giant campus that had 1,706 beds; 2.5 million square feet of patient care, educational, and research space; and 2,860 parking places. From 1962 to 1971, it would spend some $47 million on new construction, and by the

end of that period it had 3,084 employees with a payroll of slightly more than $24 million.

"So I became vice-chancellor and I started thinking, 'Why are all these hospitals moving?' I got my map and figured out that 270 was the new Kingshighway," recalls Danforth. "The neighborhood around us was running down, and people were afraid to come into the area. The question was: 'What should we do about it?' We decided to have a committee of the medical center, which consisted of most of the members of the board, and consider what we should do. One option was to

Reflection

"I lived in the neighborhood as a renter for a number of years, but I bought my home in 1970—same house I live in today. Back then, the guy representing the seller was a friend of my father's, and he tried to talk me out of buying the house. I paid under $14,000 for it. He said, 'Vince, there are three kinds of neighborhoods in St. Louis: There are black neighborhoods, there are white neighborhoods, and there are neighborhoods in transition. Black people are moving into this neighborhood, and it's going to be all black. You're going to lose your money. Don't buy here.' I went ahead and bought anyway. The Skinker-DeBaliviere neighborhood became the first truly integrated neighborhood in the city of St. Louis.

"If the university and medical center had moved out at that time, I just don't know what would have happened to the neighborhood and to the entire city, to be honest with you.

"It was a difficult neighborhood. For the first six months or so that I lived there, I was burglarized three times. It was chancy, but it was worthwhile. We look back on it now and recognize that the university and the medical center made some tough decisions, but it was really existential for the city."

—Vincent Schoemehl,
former St. Louis mayor, 1981–1993

Ronald Evens

Construction on the Medical Center campus, 1967

move—to keep up with the times and move." There was an underlying concern: the hospitals that had relocated, close to a wealthier patient base, might attract the paying patients who had previously come to Barnes.

Who should head up the effort to decide whether to stay or go? Immediately, Danforth thought of Evens, then only thirty years old but smart, sensible, and financially savvy. "I knew he was bright and able, and he was straightforward. He was not a shrinking violet, and he would get around and meet people," said Danforth. So he named Evens vice president of WUMSAH, starting in 1970, and asked him to head up a yearlong strategic planning process. "On the committee were the big shots of the hospitals, including board members," recalled Evens. "Essentially, we looked at what we thought were the best centers in the country: the Mayo Clinic, Duke, M. D. Anderson, Memorial Sloan-Kettering, the University of Texas, and others. Six or seven in our group met with key people at each place, asking them what they had done and what their plans were for the future."

This fact-finding process culminated in a one-day meeting—a debate focused on three scenarios: stay in the Central West End; move the clinical side of the campus to West County, probably to land owned by trustee George Capps that would later be occupied by Plaza Frontenac; or stay in the Central West End but build an outpatient center on the Plaza Frontenac site. Evens, who presented that last option, became its chief advocate, but another choice prevailed. "What won out was, stay here," says Evens. "Ultimately people came to the conclusion that it was best to keep all our eggs in one basket." Over the next few years, the hospitals all invested in infrastructure improvements to improve the Kingshighway location.

RAYMOND WITTCOFF AND THE FIRST PLAN

Another person passionately convinced that the Washington University Medical Center should stay in the Central West End was real estate developer Raymond H. Wittcoff, a board member of Washington University as well as the medical center. In 1979, he would be elected president of the Jewish Hospital Board of Directors, which he had already been serving as a board member. Not only was it crucial for the medical center to remain in the Central West End, he said later, but "a corollary of the decision to stay here was that we had to do something to improve the surrounding environment." In 1973, he told a *Post-Dispatch* reporter that "the future greatness of the medical center depends on its ability to attract first-rate people. First-rate people have

Raymond Wittcoff, real estate developer, Jewish Hospital board member, and city booster, undated

The HOK master plan, 1973

choices as to where they will go. The chances of getting them to come here will be improved to the extent that the environment they will live and work in will be attractive and secure. . . ."

Wittcoff had joined with Danforth and others on the committee to discuss relocation. "He was a very influential member, very bright and very articulate," said Danforth. "As a developer, he had built the first building in downtown St. Louis that had been built in twenty years. He made a very good case for staying where we were and fixing the area up—rejuvenating it. We agreed to that and were feeling good about it."

So Wittcoff contacted a friend—Gyo Obata, of the Hellmuth, Obata + Kassabaum architectural firm—to develop a plan. But their approach involved "a very urban type of development, which was totally inappropriate for the people who called the Central West End home," said Richard Roloff, a Washington University graduate and a real estate developer, who was president of Capitol Land Company. It would also require razing swaths of homes and commercial buildings.

"Ray Wittcoff asked me to do a master plan of the medical center, and we felt that the surrounding area ought also to be studied for the housing of people working there. That area was blighted in a sense, so there was the idea that we could tear down many of the buildings and put up new high-rise apartments and townhouses. We did this plan without much research into the existing fabric; it was just an idea of how to create a housing area close to the medical center. We probably should have done a lot more study. Once it was released, there was a great deal of opposition from people who lived there, and I don't blame them."

—Gyo Obata,
architect and cofounder of HOK

"When the HOK plan got in the paper, all hell broke loose. The people who lived here, the politicians who represented this area, went bonkers. 'What the hell is Washington University trying to do? This is awful. This is destroying our neighborhood. There's no consideration of the people who live here.'

"And a lot of people lived here. This was not a vacant neighborhood. It was tatty. It was run-down. It was clearly being disinvested. It didn't have an aura of success about it, that's for sure. I remember when we'd go to work in the morning, and we'd have to sweep drunks off our front steps, because there was a little bar there called Jimmy and Andy's. But it wasn't abandoned. It wasn't a wasteland.

"Yet property values had plummeted, and racial fear was profound. There were a lot of people moving out and going elsewhere. Especially along West Pine, there were rooming houses; they weren't protected by the private trust indentures, like you'd have in the private places. There were a lot of older people, who were just hanging on."

—Richard Ward,
partner in the urban design firm, Team Four

Gyo Obata, 1996

Added Richard Ward, a St. Louis urban designer, "I remember seeing it and I said, 'Holy mackerel, this is crazy!' We had just moved our office into the neighborhood, and this plan, basically, just swept the place clean. It was all new townhouses and high-rise buildings, and a complete new perspective of what the place would be."

Meanwhile, Washington University trustee George Capps, Roloff's boss at Capitol Land, suggested that Roloff would make an ideal volunteer head for the redevelopment effort. Danforth and Wittcoff took Roloff to lunch one day to persuade him to get involved. "They explained the importance of securing the neighborhood to prolong the life of the medical center, to keep the institutions together, to improve the residential areas so that people who worked at the medical center would feel comfortable living there," recalled Roloff. "They had all the right reasons. But

they also recognized the enormity of the effort that would be required."

Roloff was intrigued, despite the daunting challenge. But only a week or two after that lunch, he awoke one morning in November 1973 to see an article and map in the newspaper: the HOK plan, which someone had leaked to the paper. In the next few days, Roloff attended a neighbors' meeting on Laclede Avenue, which he thought would be a chance to get acquainted with residents. Instead, he said, "It was a lynching party in disguise. The neighbors were furious at the medical center institutions. From that picture in the paper, they had seen that their homes or properties were no longer there. The big gorilla was moving in on them, and they didn't like it. That was the sort of tone with which this whole thing got started."

The HOK plan hadn't worked—and, in fact, had made things worse. They would have to start over again. ❦

CENTRAL WEST END UPBEAT

Typical Central West End
street scene, undated

CHAPTER 5

UPBEAT AND VIBRANT

The Central West End Today

⤪ (1975–Present) ⤧

"I was impressed with the changes that had taken place here between the time I was in medical school in St. Louis during the 1970s and when I moved back in 1984. It was upbeat and vibrant, and it still afforded quiet and privacy."

—R. Morton Bolman,
heart transplant surgeon,
Washington University School of Medicine,
quoted in the *Barnes Hospital Bulletin*, 1987

The Washington University Medical Center (WUMC) had made a false start in its plan to stay and revitalize its Central West End neighborhood, but seasoned developer Richard Roloff was now heading the project—and he took another approach. "Instead of sitting down and drawing plans, Dick Roloff went around door to door talking with people, finding out what was going on, getting information," recalled William Danforth, Washington University's new chancellor in 1971, who strongly favored WUMC's decision to stay in the neighborhood. Further, Roloff hired a young, up-and-coming urban design group to spearhead the planning effort. Team Four—with principals William Albinson, Brian Kent, Jerome Pratter, and Richard Ward, along with associates Jack Pyburn and Austin Tao—had its offices in a converted police station on Newstead.

"Dick came to us and said, 'The university has made a big foul-up. We've got to find a new direction. Can you help?'" recalled Ward, whose firm had already worked on the master plan for LaSalle Park. "We said we would be glad to help, but we also said, 'We will approach it differently. We don't expect to wipe this place clean and build over. We're going to try to save as much as can be saved, repurpose as much as can be repurposed, and then surgically do new construction.'"

Calvin Stuart of the Skinker-DeBaliviere Community Council and Jerome Pratter of Team Four at a public hearing on a plan for redeveloping an area just west of the Central West End, 1972

Richard Roloff (*center*), flanked by Eddie Davis (*left*) and Julia Holmes (*right*), receiving an award from the St. Louis Minority Business Council on behalf of Washington University, 2000

Clockwise from left:
The corner of Laclede and Euclid as architects envisioned it in the future, 1977; corner of Euclid and Laclede in 1977; Barnes Hospital maintenance employees in the Town Hall restaurant, 1977; skeleton of house, 4400 Laclede, 1979

The Euclid business district with Jewish Hospital across the street, 1982

Street scene in the Central West End from the *West End Word*, undated

At first, the neighborhood was suspicious of Roloff, whose firm was then developing Plaza Frontenac, the high-end suburban plaza that was attracting some Central West End businesses to move west. "I was reminded of that frequently," said Roloff, with a chuckle. "The neighbors associated my name with the unraveling of some of the better tenancies in the Central West End. Initially, I would say that almost every resident would have bought my train ticket to California. So when I agreed to undertake the challenge, I knew it would not be easy, but I was persuaded by Bill Danforth and Ray Wittcoff that it was an important thing to do."

"The heroes of a project like this are those who see what needs to be done and try to get things going. In the early days, the first question was: Should the medical center stay where it was or move? The person who was most visionary about that was Ray Wittcoff. He gave us great leadership so that all of us were convinced that it was a good thing to stay. We were citizens of St. Louis, our institutions had grown up in St. Louis, and we felt it would be bad for the city if we all decamped to the county.

"The next question was: What do you do? The person who provided that leadership was Dick Roloff. He had been developing land with George Capps for a while, and he was very interested in how things worked, the politics, the local support or lack of support. He came down and helped us understand the community better and developed plans."

—William Danforth
chancellor of Washington University (1971–1995)

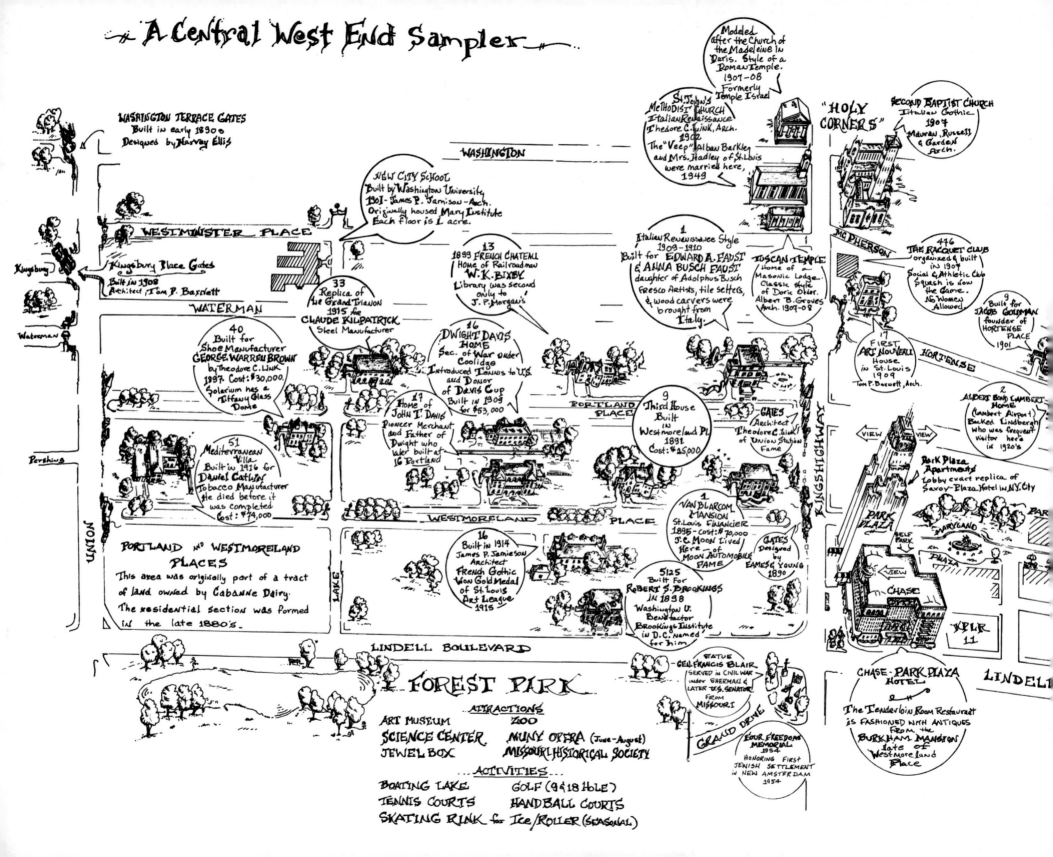

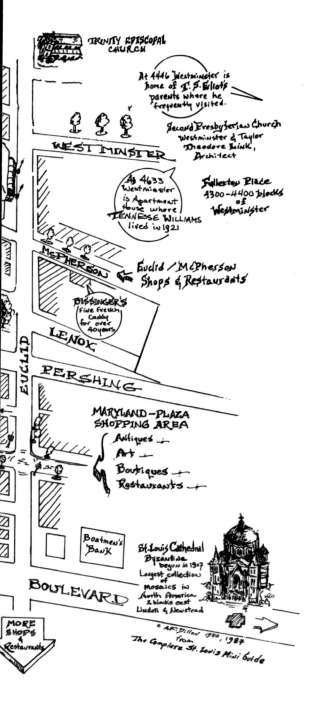

Left, Washington University Medical Center redevelopment area map, undated. *Top middle,* plans for proposed land use in redevelopment area. *Top right,* Laclede Place front yard design guide. *Bottom right,* plan for retail development of Laclede Ave., 1976.

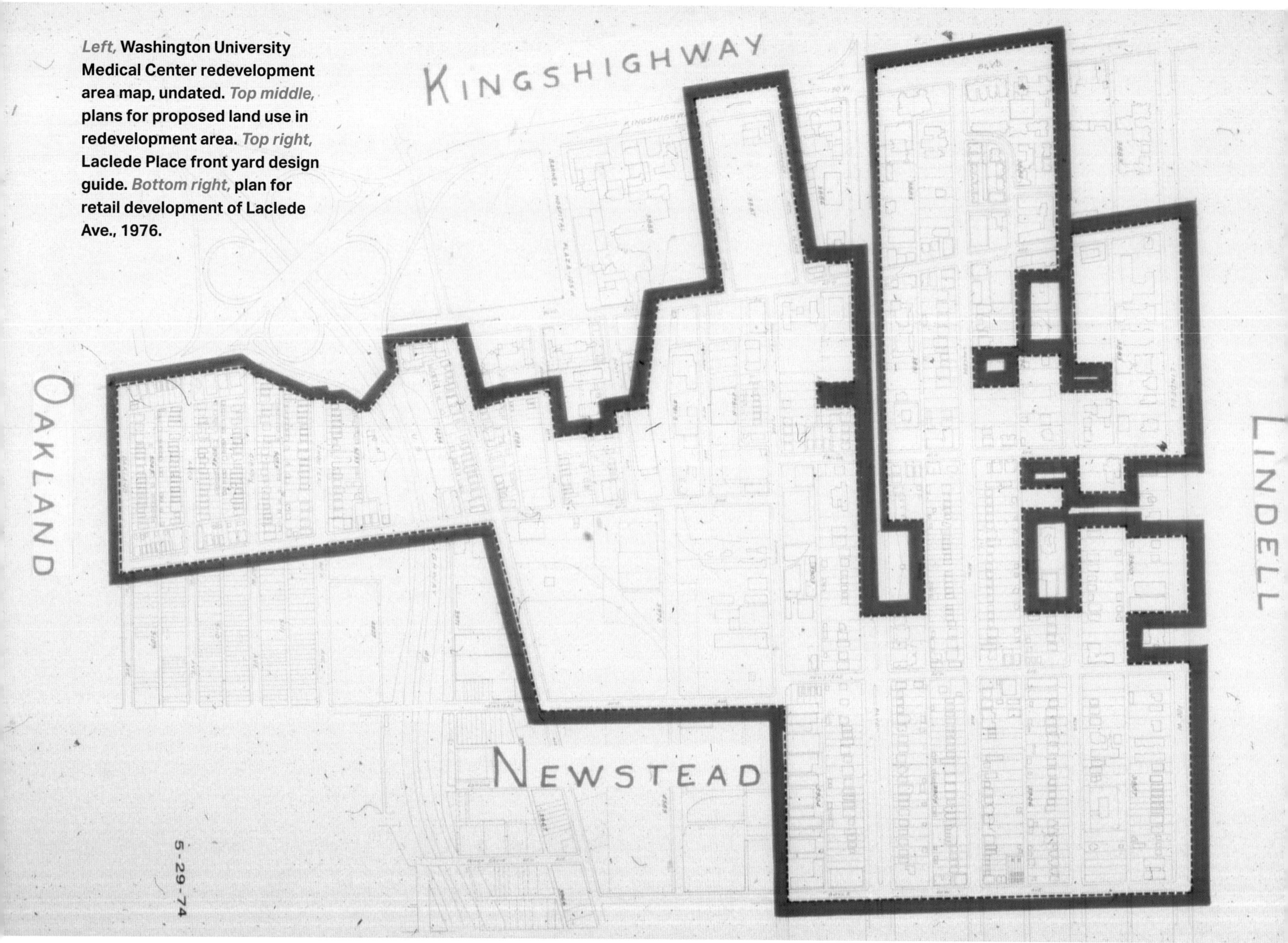

KINGSHIGHWAY

OAKLAND

LINDELL

NEWSTEAD

5-29-74

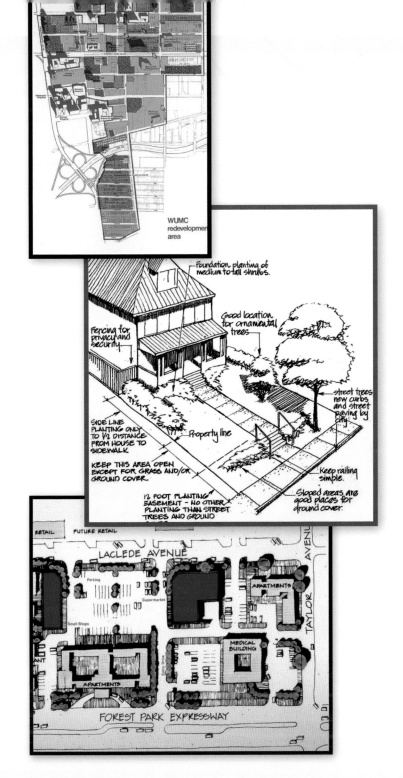

WUMC redevelopment area

Foundation planting of medium to tall shrubs.

Good location for ornamental trees

Fencing for privacy and security

street trees new curbs and street paving by city

SIDE LINE PLANTING ONLY TO 1/2 DISTANCE FROM HOUSE TO SIDEWALK

Property line

KEEP THIS AREA OPEN EXCEPT FOR GRASS AND/OR GROUND COVER.

Keep railing simple.

12 FOOT PLANTING EASEMENT - NO OTHER PLANTING THAN STREET TREES AND GROUND

Sloped areas are good places for ground cover.

RETAIL FUTURE RETAIL

LACLEDE AVENUE

TAYLOR AVENUE

Parking

APARTMENTS

Supermarket

Small Shops

MEDICAL BUILDING

Entry Drive

APARTMENTS

FOREST PARK EXPRESSWAY

THE FIRST PHASE OF REVITALIZATION

New developments began coming thick and fast. In November 1973, WUMC formed the Washington University Medical Center Redevelopment Corporation (WUMCRC), charged with creating a plan for the 185-acre target area around the medical center. The Missouri Housing Development Commission agreed to provide $30 million in low-interest mortgage money for the residential side of the project, which would cover an area roughly bounded by Oakland Avenue, Lindell Boulevard, Boyle Avenue, and Kingshighway. Then in June 1974, the city's board of aldermen passed a bill declaring that area eligible for tax benefits under the Chapter 353 Missouri Urban Redevelopment Act. In January 1975, the Team Four/WUMCRC plan was approved.

This plan aimed to reverse problems in its target area, which would be declared "blighted." According to City Plan Commission findings, verified by Team Four, only 25 percent of structures in the area were in sound condition, while 50 percent were marginal and 20 percent were substandard. Over the previous decade, both the population and property values had decreased. So the WUMCRC plan would "build on the area's many assets and critical functions, rather than allow them to be destroyed through a lack of investment and guidance in the area," it said. Rehabilitation would take place in

Central West End Tracts 1121, 1124, 1191.01, 1191.02, 1192			
	1970	1990	2015**
Population	25,859	17,282	16,134
Poverty Rate	24%	22%	21%
Per Capita Income*	$28,882.09	$43,464.95	$45,198.51
Occupancy Rate	85%	86%	86%
Percent Under 18	20%	10%	8%
Percent 18-34	28%	35%	42%
Percent Non-Hispanic White	54%	59%	56%
Percent with a 4-Year Degree	18%	45%	65%

Adjusted for inflation
ACS 2011-2015 5-year data estimates

Compiled by Todd Swanstrom and Hank Webber, and updated by Jenny Connelly-Bowen, 2017

Left, Washington University Medical Center redevelopment area "Fun Map," undated

cooperation with property owners; demolition would only occur when absolutely necessary.

In places, the plan's "action areas" were very specific. "It is proposed that [the Boulevard Apartments building] be converted back to its original use as a motel through a concerted rehabilitation program," said one piece of the plan. Laclede Avenue would be closed at Taylor and a small park created, said another. A third action area focused on the intersection of Taylor Avenue and Forest Park, where "a commercial office development . . . will be complementary to the proposed office park immediately to the south."

By the fall of 1974, a report of the WUMC president who had succeeded William Danforth—psychiatrist and vice chancellor for medical affairs Samuel Guze, who fully supported the WUMCRC initiative—took a cheerful, confident tone. The new plan, he wrote, would include "a broad selection of housing [that] would appeal to many people associated with the Medical Center, as well as the growing number of persons who prefer to live and work in the city." There would be stronger commercial areas, recreational facilities, and landscaped open spaces. Altogether, he added, "the long-range plans for the Medical Center and the massive effort to assist the neighborhood around us are bold, imaginative and vitally needed programs."

Dr. Samuel Guze (1923–2000)

NEW LIFE ON LACLEDE AVENUE

In November 1976, the *Globe-Democrat* published a story about the 4400 block of Laclede—a kind of microcosmic look at the Central West End's revitalization. "Tall and stately," said the subhead, "the old homes in the 4400 block are facing a bright new future of renovation and refurbishment."

One of the featured homes belonged to Robert E. Wentz, city public schools superintendent, and his wife, Janice. Their neighbor, Joe Mensing, had rehabilitated the badly deteriorated home and sold it to them. Another belonged to Terry and Susan Sherman, first-time city dwellers, whose home was redone by Pantheon Corporation. They still had the apartment numbers from upstairs doors to remind them of their house's period as a rooming house. It had cost $14,000 to buy, plus $36,000 to restore.

Yet another home belonged to Louis Gerteis, a history professor at the University of Missouri–St. Louis, who had bought his "shell of a house" for around $9,000 and then rehabbed it himself. Recently, he explained what made the purchase attractive and economical:

"There was a tax-abatement program associated with WUMCRC, so if you passed your deed through them and accepted their rules, you had no tax increase for the first fifteen years. There would also be certain standards: no fences in front of properties and old fire escapes would come down from when these buildings had been rooming houses. All of that gave us a sense of cohesion, and it worked. It brought the neighborhood together, and it gave me confidence that my purchase was going to be a smart one."

St. Louis Globe-Democrat Sunday Magazine photos, 1976: *facing page,* Robert Wentz home, 4400 block of Laclede; *above,* Josef Mensing looking up entry hall of Wentz home; *upper right,* kitchen in Laclede home renovated by Terry and Susan Stewart; *lower right,* Louis Gerteis standing in his unfinished kitchen on Laclede.

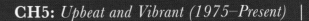

TOM'S BAR AND GRILL

Since 1976, Tom's Bar and Grill has been a neighbor-hood fixture at 20 South Euclid, and Jerry King of WUMCRC remembers how it got started. "One day, Tom Dimitriades walked in and said, 'I've got an idea. I own this little building on Euclid, and I'd like to do a bar and grill.' And we said, 'Come on in, Tom. Sit down. Let's see what we can do to help you.' Well, we helped Tom acquire another property. We introduced him to an architect. And he opened Tom's Bar and Grill.

"That was really important to us because it was a new, highly visible investment. It was a place for people from the medical center to get out into the neighbor-hood, to cross Forest Park. And Tom? I'll never forget it. This is hard to believe but I think it cost him around $80,000 to put this deal together, which is nothing.

"About ten months later, he walked into our office, handing out cigars. He was celebrating the fact that he had made the last payment on his $80,000 loan. He had already turned enough profit that he could pay off his loan. For us, that was a signal achievement—to have a new restaurant and bar that was very successful."

Tom's Bar and Grill

Left to right, **Jerry Pratter, Richard Ward, and William Albinson are three originals from Team Four.**

But some residents were still skeptical. A *Post-Dispatch* article in September 1974 described a meeting of Team Four and Roloff with some two hundred property owners to discuss the plan—and particularly its blighting provision, which would give the developer the power of eminent domain. "Why did you declare this area blighted when the city as a whole is in worse condition than this area?" wrote Tom Mezines of 4449 Laclede in a letter to the board of aldermen on behalf of residents.

"We did have a lot of public meetings," said Ward. "Dick was outstanding at running them; I always admired his coolness. I would be all antsy and upset about things people were saying, but Dick let people have their say. I think we did it right. Dick was firm, wanting to move forward, and he wasn't going to be easily deterred, but he gave everybody an opportunity to be heard."

"WHERE SHOULD I SIGN?"

Meanwhile, Roloff's own energetic teammates were interviewing residents to find out who wanted to sell their homes. Richard Lahr, then a student and later mayor of Des Peres, needed a summer job, and he began going door to door; so did WUMCRC staff member Sharon Archibald. "They got a pretty clear message that the area had become unattractive

Mayor James Conway (*left*) and Washington University chancellor William H. Danforth, and his wife Ibby tour the renovated commercial area, 1978.

as a place to live," said Roloff. "One of their questions was, 'would [the owners] be interested in selling their home if we could find a buyer?' There was a strong response of people who just wanted out. I then followed up and negotiated a lot of the purchases. I remember one extremely large brick home—it must have been five or six thousand square feet—and an elderly lady lived there alone. All she wanted to know was 'where should I sign?'"

Once WUMCRC acquired a property, the staff would find a builder or developer who would buy it—with the understanding that it could not be demolished

without approval, and it would undergo a high-quality rehabbing. In the case of most single-family houses, buyers bought them directly and undertook their own renovations. If residents needed help relocating, WUMCRC would provide it.

This project was expensive, and WUMC institutions agreed to contribute according to a fixed formula. Then, "we went to Civic Progress and asked those companies to buy bonds," recalled Danforth. "We would pay 6 percent interest. And they did it. But most Civic Progress companies put the bonds into their charitable trusts and gave them away, thinking they

**Joseph Roddy Sr.
(1919–2005)**

Jerry King

would never get repaid. But we repaid all the bonds." Overall, said Roloff—who was himself uncompensated, though he still had paid employment at Capitol Land, which strongly supported his Central West End work—"we operated on a shoestring. Everybody was in it for the good of the medical center."

They also needed support from politicians, and the influential alderman from Gibson Heights (later Forest Park Southeast), Joseph Roddy Sr., provided key help. "He went above and beyond the call of duty," added Roloff. "He saw the need for what we were trying to do, and when he thought something was appropriate, he would go to bat and move it forward." In fact, Roddy liked the plan well enough that he wanted to extend the redevelopment south of the highway. Finally, the WUMCRC board agreed to add six square blocks to their focus area.

"RUNNING SHOES"

In February 1975, just after the redevelopment plans were approved, WUMCRC hired an executive director, Jerry King, who came with strong experience in real estate investment and development. The timing of his appointment was no accident: he had told Roloff that he wouldn't take the job unless the aldermen approved the redevelopment plan and

"My dad was elected alderman in 1953 and appointed circuit clerk in 1968. Neighborhoods were closer then because people didn't move as much. Everybody knew who was out of a job or down on their luck. Most of the women worked in their homes. If one of them lost her husband, the neighborhood would come together to help her out. She might end up working at city hall, and a Christmas basket would show up at her house. It was a more close-knit community, I think.

"For a redevelopment project, there are all kinds of enabling things the city can provide to help out: economic incentives, use of eminent domain, zoning. Of course, people still have to be informed through public hearings. So my dad's role was very much as an intermediary. At neighborhood meetings, people would jump up and start yelling at leaders from the medical center who were explaining what was going on. My dad would know the people on a first-name basis, so he would say, 'Now calm down. We all have to get through this and listen to each other.'

"By creating space for those dialogues, an element of trust developed, and eventually the legislation would get passed. With his nudging, he also dragged the redevelopment area to expand south of the highway. Initially they were reluctant, but over time they realized it was important for them strategically to support that neighborhood as well."

—Joseph Roddy Jr.,
alderman for the Seventeenth Ward,
whose father was circuit clerk for the same neighborhood

Blue Cross Building Called Big Step In West End Redevelopment

By FRANDO J. WEBB
Of the Post-Dispatch Staff

The near completion of the multimillion-dollar Blue Cross headquarters building in the 4200 block of Forest Park Avenue represents a major achievement for the Washington University Medical School Redevelopment Corporation, says the corporation's executive director.

R. Jerrad King told about 100 persons at a meeting of the Central West End Association this week that the building would lend credibility to the corporation's plan to redevelop a large area in the city's Central West End. The meeting was held at the Knight's of Columbus Hall, 4331 Lindell Boulevard.

"By October, more than 1000 employes will be moving into that building," King said.

The corporation plans to develop an area bounded roughly by Lindell on the north, Boyle Avenue on the east, Oakland Avenue on the south, and Kingshighway on the west.

About a year ago, the city granted the corporation tax advantages and the right of eminent domain to undertake the nine-year project, which will cover about 36 blocks. The corporation's backers, six west end medical institutions, have so far committed about $2,000,000 to the project, he said.

The plans include building town houses, rehabiliting old houses and constructing a 240-unit housing facility for the elderly.

King said that some structures that were to have been demolished were now being considered for renovation.

And others scheduled for renovation now are in the line-up for demolition, he said.

"For example, the Lindell Plaza Hotel and other structures in that area were going to be torn down," he said. "But now we're going to develop them into some apartments.

"The 4300 block of Laclede is the only area that is sched-uled for full block demolition, which will allow for the construction of town houses," King said.

The corporation plans to acquire the 45 buildings in the 4400 block of Laclede Avenue and make it into a private street. So far, 11 of the buildings have been acquired and three persons have made commitments to purchase and renovate houses, he said.

King said he did not foresee any difficulties for individuals in getting financing to renovate the houses.

"Banks and savings and loan institutions are anxious to provide the backing because they have, in the past, been accused of red-lining certain portions of the city," King said. "Red-lining" is the refusal of lending institutions to lend in neighborhoods they considered declining.

King insisted that the program was based on maintaining as much of the character and diversity of the area as possible. Most of the commercial establishments will be neighborhood-oriented, he said.

"The shops will have the butcher, the baker and the candlestick-maker concept," he said.

St. Louis Post-Dispatch, **January 29, 1976**

the WUMC institutions agreed to provide funding. Then Roloff called to say that both things had happened—was he interested? "I got off the phone after talking to him and I said to my wife, 'I got offered the medical center redevelopment job,' and she said, 'great! What's the salary?' And I said, 'Oh! I was so excited that I forgot to ask!'"

When he arrived, he had a first meeting with Roloff and found that the project had just gotten more complicated. "He said, 'You better have your running shoes on, because we've signed a contract with Blue Cross Blue Shield to deliver a fourteen-acre site [for their new headquarters building] on the south side of Forest Park Avenue by July.'" In an unheard-of five months' time, King and his small staff—mainly Archibald and new assistant director Eugene Kilgen,

a planner and real estate consultant—had to acquire twenty-eight properties, move a sewer line, relocate tenants, install a left-turn signal and streetlights, and make intersection improvements at Newstead and Forest Park, which involved closing Newstead for a time. Some houses along Forest Park had to be demolished. The old City Ice and Fuel plant disappeared; so did an old firehouse with the traditional handball court outside.

"During that period, Sharon walked in one day, and she was white as a sheet," recalled King. "She sat down in my office and I said, 'What in the world is wrong?' She had gone to see a vacant boardinghouse property that we were thinking of purchasing, and encountered a dead body at the bottom of the staircase. Those were the kinds of properties we were looking at."

GONE: THE SAN LUIS APARTMENTS

In 1961, *Post-Dispatch* headlines announced plans for an eleven-story, $4.5 million luxury motor hotel at 4483 Lindell to be built by developers Melvin and Harold Dubinsky. "The E-shaped structure, with a 12-story central wing and two six-story wings, will be known as the St. Louis De Ville," said the story. The 226-room hotel, the "first major hotel constructed in St. Louis since the Park Plaza was built in 1929," would occupy a site where "three large residences had recently stood."

But only five years later, the inn became the Holiday Inn–Midtown motel. Then in 1974, the St. Louis Archdiocese applied for funds from the Department of Housing and Urban Development to convert it to a residence for the elderly. In 1975, they began taking applications for the 226-unit San Luis Apartments, managed by the Cardinal Ritter Institute. Some problems ensued. In 1982, a woman was beaten and robbed as she was leaving for mass at the St. Louis Cathedral, and in 1983 there was a fire at the facility.

San Luis Apartments, 4483 Lindell, 1975

In 2007, residents were relocated from the motel, which the archdiocese wanted to demolish and replace with a parking lot. Despite a campaign to save the mid-century modern high-rise, it was torn down in 2008.

A view of the new Monsanto building's Clayton Avenue facade, with three stacks to handle the building's exhaust, 1978

The Monsanto building in the Central West End, 1983

Despite intense efforts, they delivered the Blue Cross property a bit late—but the company was still able to break ground on the facility, which today is the School of Medicine's 4444 Building. They worked with Leon Strauss of Pantheon to develop Park Place, a $6 million, 240-unit senior citizen complex designed by Eugene Mackey Associates at Forest Park and Newstead. They promoted construction of Monsanto's elegant, $12.5 million Environmental Health Laboratory at Clayton and Newstead, which won an award from the American Institute of Architects. At the same time, they began focusing on the 4400 block of Laclede, called Laclede Place.

All the while, the community was staying in touch with their progress. "We were asked to make presentations to community groups, so we would show them the plan and what had happened so far. Everybody kept close track of how many new dollars were being invested in the neighborhood," said King. He put together an informal, unpaid group of architects and planners—from Team Four, HOK, Peckham Guyton, and others—to do design reviews of new construction. And he reported frequently to the WUMCRC executive committee, headed by Samuel Guze, who was deeply involved in decision-making, along with members Danforth, Wittcoff, and Roloff.

After two years on the job, King ran into a rough patch. Amid slow-moving acquisition talks between Jewish Hospital and a property owner on Euclid, a key medical practice with a suite in the building got fed up and moved west. King, who had brokered the negotiations, "took the heat on that, so in October 1977, I decided to resign." Replacing the fast-moving, decisive King was Kilgen, his second-in-command and polar opposite. Once a Jesuit seminarian, he was thoughtful and visionary. Suzanne Goodman (later Sherman), who joined the WUMCRC team in 1978, said that Kilgen "knew the rules and stayed within the rules. The medical center wanted to remain in the city, but if they didn't have a safe and secure neighborhood, they weren't going to stay. Gene really took that to heart."

Under his leadership, the work continued, including property acquisition. "One day, I went down on Boyle to talk to a German woman who owned a big, three-story building, and she was living in a tiny room in the back," said Sherman. "She had some bums living there as well. We sat at her kitchen table and talked about Germany, about her plans. She said she wanted to get out, and if we'd buy her building, she'd be very happy. Sometimes you couldn't just walk in and say, 'We want to buy your building.' You had to build a relationship."

Central West End street in spring, undated

Gene Kilgen of the Washington University Medical Center Redevelopment Corporation, 1983

Houses slated for redevelopment, 1988

"CONCERTED EFFORT" PAYS OFF

But making real progress took time, and along the way, some people were critical. In 1979, *Post-Dispatch* interior design reporter Patricia Degener wrote a review of the Central West End project that pointed out some of its less-than-successful aspects. "About $1.5 million in public money has been spent to date on improvements in the WUMCRC area, but the concepts behind the improvements outshine the execution." On the 4400 block of Laclede, she said, were poorly chosen plantings in the center island and a proliferation of concrete knickknacks at Laclede and Euclid. The trash cans "should be awarded some kind of prize for disastrous design."

Yet as time went on, said Art Perry, "there was a ripple effect from the Washington University redevelopment: a little more confidence in the ownership of homes and property all the way to Westminster. To be associated with the medical center was a real positive thing. Young doctors, as well as some staff and educators from Hilltop campus, moved into our area. At one point in the years from 1980 on, half the homes must have had doctors, lawyers, and judges between Taylor and Euclid on Westminster. You couldn't go six houses without hitting one of those professions."

In 1987, a *Barnes Hospital Bulletin* article named many employees who had bought homes in the Central West End, such as respiratory therapist Lamont Estes,

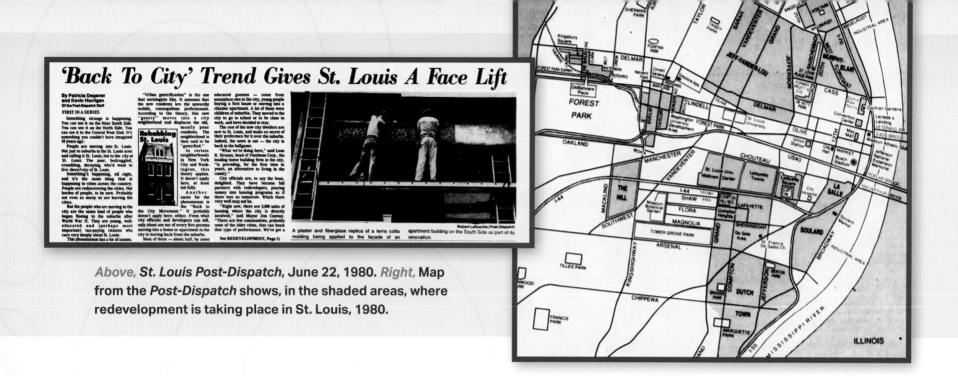

Above, *St. Louis Post-Dispatch*, June 22, 1980. *Right,* Map from the *Post-Dispatch* shows, in the shaded areas, where redevelopment is taking place in St. Louis, 1980.

who called it "the best place in the city." Only ten years earlier, continued the story, a WUMCRC official had said, "There are 10,000 people in the medical center across Forest Park Boulevard, but only a few of them cross the intersection each day to spend time and money in the Euclid-Laclede area." Now all that had changed, said the story. "'Stimulating,' 'convenient' and 'fabulous' are just a few of the words Barnes employees use to describe their homes in the Central West End neighborhood."

In their 2014 report on "Rebound Neighborhoods" of St. Louis, authors Todd Swanstrom and Hank Webber gave credit for the area's successful revitalization to "the institutional and civic forces . . . [that] responded to the challenges facing the neighborhood with skill and dedication. While there was much they could not control, many groups in the Central West End worked effectively to promote the neighborhood and capitalize on its strengths." But they also added that "the single largest factor contributing to the CWE's success was the decision of Washington University's School of Medicine, the Central Institute for the Deaf, and Barnes, Jewish, and Children's Hospitals to remain in place and launch a concerted effort to improve the surrounding neighborhoods."

Top left, Washington University Medical Center, 1981. *Top right,* Jewish Hospital, early 1980s. *Bottom left,* architect's drawing, new St. Louis Children's Hospital, 1980s. *Inset,* William H. Danforth speaking at the dedication of the Washington University School of Medicine's Clinical Sciences Research Building, October 17, 1984. *Bottom right,* St. Louis Children's Hospital groundbreaking, November 10, 1980: *left to right,* William Danforth, James McDonnell III, Linn Perkins, James Conway, Alvin Tolin, Philip Dodge.

Sidewalk sales at the Euclid Jubilee, 1978

The Euclid Jubilee, with the now-demolished Ettrick Building in the background, at the corner of Euclid and Forest Park, 1978

EVENTS AND VISITORS

Meanwhile, the area was hosting visitors as well as festive events, some planned by the Central West End Merchants Association. Through the late 1970s, the Central West End celebrated annual Christmas walks, an outgrowth of the earlier Sunday gallery walks, with caroling, Greek and Russian pastries, Rosati-Kain singers, Bissinger's candies, even appearances by Santa Claus. Bob Kramer's Marionnettes, a neighborhood fixture with its popular puppetry theater on Laclede, also performed. The annual Halloween Party had also grown from some 11,500 participants in 1980 to 50,000 in 1983; the Taste of the Central West End, with music, art, and food, began in 1991; and in 2014, the Central West End House Tour celebrated its forty-fourth year.

Author A. E. Hotchner's memoir-turned-film, *King of the Hill*, which captured Hotchner's boyhood experiences living by his wits in a cheap hotel during the Depression, was shot largely in the Central West End during a steamy eight-week period in the summer of 1993. The exterior of the hotel, which actually had been the Westgate at Kingshighway and Delmar, was the Lister Building at North Taylor and Olive. Hotchner's school, the Dewey School, was portrayed by the New City School at Lake and Waterman. The movie also showed the exterior of various local apartments, including the Sherwood Courts.

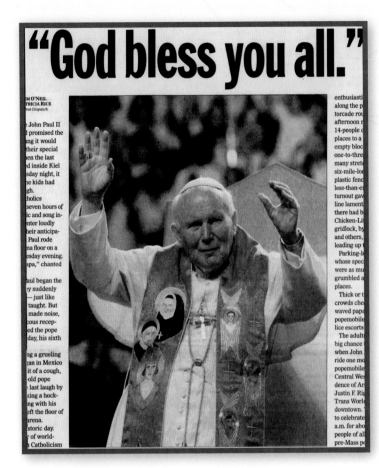

Newspaper clipping headline: **"God bless you all."**

Pope John Paul II on his visit to St. Louis,
St. Louis Post-Dispatch, January 27, 1999

In 1999, Central West End residents joined others across St. Louis in celebrating the visit of Pope John Paul II, who traveled a six-mile stretch of Lindell and Olive in his bubble-topped Mercedes on his way to Archbishop Justin Rigali's home on Lindell. But well-wishers along the route were sparser than expected, after media warnings about traffic and huge crowds persuaded some people to stay home.

Through the years, the neighborhood attracted its own share of characters. Until he left town for Atlanta in 2004, "Baton Bob" Jamerson was one of them. Regularly, he appeared on Central West End streets, especially on Euclid, wearing glitzy tiaras or frothy tutus and twirling his trademark baton.

GAY PRIDE IN THE CENTRAL WEST END

For many years, gay residents had been making an important contribution to the life of the Central West End. In 1977, Alderman Mary Stolar praised the gays and lesbians living in her Twenty-Fifth Ward, calling them an asset to the area and citing their willingness to rehabilitate old housing. Said one June 1977 article in the *Post-Dispatch*, "discothèques such as Herbie's and bars like The Potpourri cater to male homosexuals and gawking 'straights.' Other bars, like the

Onyx Room Bar, 3560 Olive Street, cater to black homosexuals, and still others, like the Bottom of the Pot, in the basement of The Potpourri, to female homosexuals."

In 1975, a group of Christians, most of them gay, began meeting in a converted house at 5108 Waterman Boulevard formerly owned by the St. Louis Theosophical Society. By 1984, when it moved to South St. Louis, the Metropolitan Community Church of Greater St. Louis had grown to about 130 active members. In June 1986, at least six hundred people marched through the Central West End in the seven-year-old Gay Pride parade, which ended with a picnic in Forest Park. "It's gay pride, and that's what the whole thing is about. It's a celebration," said Joel Hershey, president of the St. Louis Lesbian and Gay Pride Celebration Committee. During the 1999 parade, participants reflected on progress since the first parade in 1980, when some marchers wore masks, afraid of repercussions at work or in their families.

In 1997, mayoral candidates gathered at Trinity Episcopal Church to seek the support of gay and lesbian groups in the upcoming election. As *Post-Dispatch* columnist Greg Freeman wrote, the Central West End was the logical venue for such an event, because "the racially mixed central corridor is generally believed to be more liberal than other parts of the city and generally thought to have a higher gay

Newspaper articles celebrating the Gay Pride parades of 1986 (*top*) and 1994 (*bottom*)

Paraquad van, undated

Max Starkloff

and lesbian population." Kris Kleindienst of Left Bank Books mentioned the spirit of creativity in community life, "much of it made possible by the gay community," she said. "Many shop owners were gay, and many of the people who supported the neighborhood were gay. That energy was what sustained this place over a long time."

HELPING THOSE IN NEED

Another key aspect of community life was the remarkable number of organizations in the area devoted to helping the disabled and physically or mentally ill. One of them was Paraquad, founded by Max Starkloff, who was confined to a wheelchair after suffering debilitating injuries in a car accident. In 1970, he began looking for ways to leave a nursing home, and in 1975 he bought a home in the Central West End. But along the way, he also discovered a broader need for accessible housing and founded Paraquad, located at first on Laclede Avenue. A series of successes followed: the first curb cuts in St. Louis, the first lift-equipped public buses, the founding of new programs for youth and family, employment, and public policy. Starkloff and his wife, Colleen, received the Distinguished Service Award from President George H. W. Bush in 1991.

In 1979, Gini Laurie and her small staff, which included her husband, Joseph, celebrated the twentieth anniversary of her annual publication, the *Rehabilitation Gazette*, created in her Central West End home. Laurie, whose own family had suffered losses years earlier in the polio epidemic, began the *Gazette* as a newsletter to let polio survivors know about medical advances and products that would make their lives easier. But it grew into a magazine with a circulation of some forty thousand in 1989 that also featured stories about the courage and success of people with disabilities.

"Housing, Faith, Hope" is the motto of Doorways, a nonprofit organization founded in 1988 by an interfaith group of clergy, which provides stable, affordable housing for individuals and families with HIV/AIDS while also improving access to healthcare and social services. A special focus of the program—located at 4385 Maryland Avenue, once the home of the Methodist Orphans' Home Association and later the Bernard Nursing Home—is to care for the community's homeless. Doorways became the first organization in Missouri to offer housing, food, social services, and twenty-four-hour support to seriously ill AIDS patients.

In 1974, a *Post-Dispatch* story said, "psychoanalysis is alive and well and flourishing in St. Louis." Home base for this discipline was the St. Louis Psychoanalytic Institute at

Joe and Gini Laurie, 1983

Dr. Alex Kaplan

Some members of the Independence Center, 1983

4525 Forest Park, which began as the St. Louis Psychoanalytic Foundation in 1956. It was approved as an independent training institute in 1974, and right away six students entered the program. The medical director of the institute was Alex Kaplan, who had headed psychiatry at Jewish Hospital from 1958 to 1966.

In 1981, some parents from the Alliance for the Mentally Ill joined forces to found the Independence Center, a psychiatric center aimed at rehabilitating its clientele, mostly young adults with schizophrenia. Those members would socialize but also work: preparing lunch, performing clerical tasks, or helping out in its thrift store. Among its other facilities today are a clubhouse, established in 2007 at 4245 Forest Park, and a number of independent housing communities with round-the-clock support.

CRIME CONTINUES TO DEAL BLOWS TO NEIGHBORHOOD

Despite all the successes, crime—and occasionally violent crime—continued to plague the Central West End. In 1983, Washington Terrace homeowner Colette Gill was murdered by an intruder, along with her four-year-old daughter, Tiffany. In 1989, thirty-five-year-old Peter McGuire was shot in the head during a street robbery in the 4600 block of McPherson. In the same year, police said that in their Ninth District, which includes part of the Central West End, the number of murders had decreased from forty-seven in 1979 to eight in 1989, and that crime in the city had gone up by 10 percent, though only 3 percent in the Central West End. But residents questioned these statistics at a public meeting, talking of repeated break-ins and muggings.

The 1990s saw still more violence. In 1995, architect Jeffrey Krewson was shot and killed on Lake Avenue during an attempted carjacking. His two children and wife, Lyda, later the Twenty-Eighth Ward alderman and in 2017 elected mayor, were also in the car. Later, James Wade was convicted of the killing. In 1996, retired educator Frederick Stark, age eighty-three, was beaten and strangled in his home in the 4700 block of Westminster.

During the first decade of the twenty-first century, the Central West End suffered a scourge of downspout robberies. One 2006 newspaper story told of a city police officer, at home in the 4300 block of Westminster following his night shift, who awoke in the afternoon to find a man in his backyard, stealing his copper downspout. The officer tried to arrest the culprit, and during the ensuing struggle, the man was shot in the leg. There were also murders. In 2012, Saint Louis University volleyball standout Megan Boken was on her cell phone when she was shot to death during a robbery attempt. A network of ninety-one new security cameras was installed by April 2013.

VYING FOR THE FOREST PARK HOTEL

In 1994, followers of the Maharishi Mahesh Yogi paid $550,000 for the seventy-one-year-old, 200-room Forest Park Hotel at 4906 West Pine. The building, vacant for four years, had been designed by Preston Bradshaw, who also designed the Chase Hotel. A seven-story addition by George Barnett

Lyda Krewson, *St. Louis Post-Dispatch* March 31, 2017

Top left, **The entrance to the vacant Forest Park Hotel. The WUMCRC filed suit to take control of the seventy-five-year-old landmark, 1998.** *Bottom left,* **The interior of Herschel's, the Forest Park Hotel's all-night restaurant, pictured here during the renovation of the hotel into apartments, 2001.** *Right,* **The newly renovated Residences at Forest Park Hotel, 2003.**

went up in 1926. The maharishi and his Maharishi Vedic University in North Carolina wanted to revamp it as a hotel and university devoted to transcendental meditation, and in 1997 some reports said that interior renovations had begun.

But by late 1997, there were rumors that WUMCRC might be interested in taking over the hotel by eminent domain. That October, after attempting unsuccessfully to purchase it from the maharishi, WUMCRC did attempt to gain control, complaining that the maharishi and his adherents hadn't renovated the building or reopened it as promised, and that it needed some $3 million in repairs. As the suit put it, the building remains "vacant, unimproved, and a decaying behemoth in an otherwise vibrant neighborhood."

The judge ruled in favor of WUMCRC, which had the right to oversee development in the area. The maharishi appealed and lost, and WUMCRC paid $680,000 for the property. In 2000, the Westin Group bought the hotel and began a $25 million renovation, supported in part by the AFL-CIO's Housing Investment Fund, to accommodate some 115 studio, one- and two-bedroom rental apartments. The one-story addition came down to make room for outdoor dining. The new incarnation of the hotel was called "The Residences at Forest Park Hotel," and a new restaurant, the 1764 Public House, opened there in 2016.

CHASE PARK PLAZA

By 1980, beset by competition from newer suburban hotels, the Chase Park Plaza was struggling. On the Chase side, there were few "good rooms." Harold Koplar admitted that nearly half of the seven hundred rooms had deteriorated, and that occupancy was down to 40 percent. Starting in 1977, Koplar Enterprises could not pay its tax bill, but Harold Koplar still tried, with no luck, to attract $6.8 million in loans to renovate the hotel. Reluctantly, he put his beloved hotel on the market, and in 1981 he had an offer from Howard Fink, head of Town Management Corporation of Chicago, plus a consortium of other investors, including St. Louis architect Paul Londe. In May, he signed a contract to sell the Chase, Park Plaza, Chester Apartments, and garage. He would not sell the Chase Apartments on Lindell, where the successful KPLR–Channel 11, a television station that had begun broadcasting in 1959, had its studio.

In 1983, GE Capital of Connecticut, a subsidiary of General Electric, bought the complex and spent $12 million to renovate the Park Plaza. But in 1989, with only 25 percent of its rooms in use, they shut down the hotel. Despite its problems, that closing hit many hard, including surgeon Jacob Probstein, who had lived in the Park Plaza for twenty years and practiced medicine from an office in the Chase.

Upper left, **artist's rendering of Maryland Plaza with the Chase Park Plaza in the background;** *lower left,* **St. Louis Post-Dispatch**, 1979; *right,* **Maryland Plaza fountain in 2011**

KPLR–CHANNEL 11

On April 28, 1959, Cardinals baseball appeared on television screens around St. Louis, broadcast by a new independent station: KPLR–Channel 11. Its call letters came from the last name of its owner, Harold Koplar, and this station, the latest of Koplar's many projects, was the product of his entrepreneurial spirit.

In its programming, KPLR had notable successes, such as *The Three Stooges*, a hit with kids, and *Wrestling at the Chase*, an improbable mixture of brute force and elegance with Joe Garagiola as ring announcer. Even Sam Koplar would come down from his apartment in the Park Plaza to watch it. Harry Fender became "Captain 11" on *Captain 11's Showboat*.

In the mid-1960s, Harold's son Ted joined the station as a producer and sports director, and in 1979 his father named him president of 220 Television Inc. In 1998, Koplar Communications Inc. sold the broadcast license for KPLR-TV to Acme Television Holdings LLC for $150 million.

Putting the finishing touches on renovations to the Chase's lounge, *St. Louis Post-Dispatch*, March 18, 1999

"They're going to close the place; it makes you sick," he said in a story in that year. Most of the hotel's furnishings and fittings—artwork, antiques, china, pianos, light fixtures, bedroom sets, even mouthwash—were sold in 1991.

Happily, a group of investors and developers, Kingsdell L.P., bought the Chase Park Plaza in 1997 and began a giant $70 million renovation of the Chase and adjacent Chester Apartments. In 1999, headlines read: "St. Louis Landmark Reopens for Business." The Chase Park Plaza was back, beautifully renovated; craftsmen had restored such details as the ornate plasterwork in the lobby. On the Park Plaza side, there were luxury condominiums, and on the Chase side were restaurants, a refurbished Khorassan Room, a five-screen movie theater, and a stylish fitness center.

Rendering of the proposed Central West End synagogue, Central Reform, 1996

NEWCOMERS TO THE NEIGHBORHOOD

As part of the neighborhood revitalization, an exciting new wave of businesses and nonprofits came to the area. In 1999, groundbreaking ceremonies took place for a 25,000-square-foot branch library at Lindell and Euclid, named for longtime library supporters and civic leaders Daniel and Adelaide Schlafly.

Central Reform Congregation, founded in 1984 by ten families, had been holding services for years in the First Unitarian Church at Waterman and Kingshighway under the leadership of Rabbi Susan Talve. As the congregation grew, it began planning in the mid-1990s to buy the site of the onetime Diplomat Motel, later used for Section 8 senior citizen housing,

just across the street. In 1999, the community broke ground on its 22,500-square-foot synagogue called Sukkat Shalom ("Shelter of Peace")—the first to be built in any city nationally, except New York, since the 1970s—which today serves 750 households.

In 2002, Third Degree Glass Factory opened as a glass-blowing studio and events venue in a 1930s car dealership and service station at 5200 Delmar—in one newspaper story, owner Jim McKelvey called the site "a dilapidated, toxic mess"—with the help of $75,000 in state tax credits. That money made possible the purchase of furnaces, ventilation equipment, and a forklift to move pallets of glass for the 8,000-square-foot facility, which has since thrived as a glass art education center.

Bowood Farms, based in Clarksville, Missouri, had

Glass blowers at Third Degree Glass Factory, 2003

A chef at Café Osage cuts herbs from the rooftop at Bowood Farms, Olive and Walton, 2008.

long been a wholesale perennial grower there, but they decided to open a retail location in St. Louis. Owners John and Connie McPheeters, who had lived in the Central West End in the '70s and '80s, found a dilapidated 1920s-era warehouse—originally built as an auto body garage, later used for plastics and cabinet manufacturing—at the corner of Olive and Walton and began rehabbing it in 2005. Soon they added Café Osage for breakfast and lunches. John McPheeters won the mayor's Spirit of St. Louis Award in 2006 for expansion to the city and establishing retail space in the Central West End.

The World Chess Hall of Fame, founded in 1984, moved to St. Louis from Miami in 2011 with the financial backing of philanthropist Rex Sinquefield, a Central West End resident himself, who also renovated a building on Maryland for its permanent collection and temporary exhibits. Across the street, the Chess Club and Scholastic Center of St. Louis (CCSCSL)—a three-level, 6,000-square-foot center featuring a large tournament hall—opened in 2008 through Sinquefield's support. In 2014, the US Senate named St. Louis the National Chess Capital for its work in promoting chess.

World Chess Hall of Fame, 2015

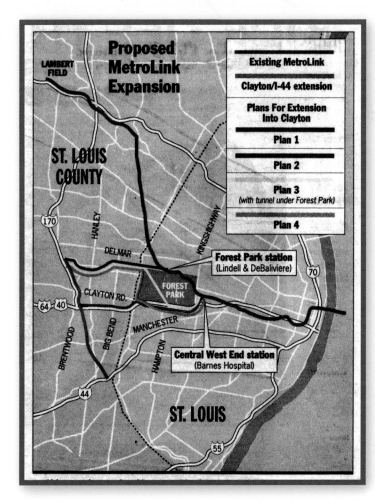

Map of proposed new MetroLink lines, *St. Louis Post-Dispatch*, 1996

METROLINK PROVIDES TRANSPORTATION

Since the nineteenth century, various forms of transportation—the Wabash Railroad, horsecar lines, streetcars, and buses—had crisscrossed the neighborhood. From 1926 to 1933, historic Route 66 also ran on parts of Lindell, turning south at Skinker toward Manchester Road. In 1993, an eighteen-mile stretch of a new, $351-million light-rail system, which had opened on July 31, was having strong early success. "The popularity of MetroLink has surprised supporters and naysayers alike," said the *Post-Dispatch*. There had been a million riders in the first five weeks alone, with some 30,000 riders a day; transit officials had predicted there would initially be 10,000–12,000.

Along the route, which extended from East St. Louis to Lambert Field, several stops were located in and around the Central West End. In 2006, after considerable debate over its route, St. Louis marked the opening of a new MetroLink extension that would run from the Central West End to Shrewsbury, going underground at the Skinker intersection. Its total price tag, with cost overruns, was a hefty $678 million. In 2015, the Sunnen station was the least used of the thirty-seven Metrolink stops, but the Central West End

Photos of Forest Park before renovation: *Left,* the World's Fair Pavilion; *right,* the Jewel Box

station at the intersection of Euclid and Children's Place—which continues to serve the Washington University Medical Center—was the busiest, with average monthly boardings of 140,060. In 2014, a pickup truck hit a train coming into the Central West End station, injuring twenty-one people.

FOREST PARK IS REBORN

By the early 1990s, the centerpiece of St. Louis—the 1,300-acre Forest Park—was looking shabby and worn. But the nonprofit Forest Park Forever, which works in partnership with the city to maintain the park, developed a comprehensive master plan that included new bike trails and major work to such key features as the Jewel Box, the Grand Basin, and the Boathouse. Other areas of the park—Kennedy Woods, the baseball fields, the golf courses—also underwent restoration. This work, carried out from 1995 to 2003, cost $94 million, and St. Louisans from all economic strata contributed to it. In 1999, Forest Park Forever even launched a successful "Pennies for the Park" campaign that attracted donations from 170 groups, among them retirement homes, Rotary Clubs, churches, Scouts, and elementary school classes. Altogether, said the *Post-Dispatch,* the restoration project was "one of St. Louis' greatest achievements of the past 50 years."

Photos of Forest Park before renovation: *Above,* the Jewel Box, undated; *left insets,* the Grand Basin

Facing page, Government Hill and the World's Fair Pavilion; *top left,* Highlands Golf Course; *middle left,* the Grand Basin; *bottom left,* bicyclist on the new dual-lane bike path; *right,* the Jewel Box

Other major projects followed, such as the $4 million reconstruction of the slope, staircases, and fountain of Government Hill. Later, local philanthropists stepped in to secure the park's future. In 2015, the Taylor family donated $30 million to Forest Park Forever to maintain the park, while James S. and Elizabeth Hall McDonnell, along with the JSM Charitable Trust, made a gift of $20 million.

Meanwhile, events enjoyed by many St. Louisans began or continued. The Horseless Carriage Club held its annual Easter Sunday Concours d'Elegance in Forest Park with an array of beautifully restored antique cars. Earth Day Festivals took place in May, while a seasonal shuttle operated during the high-visitor period. Among the best-loved events was the annual fall Great Forest Park Balloon Race, which began in 1973, along with its companion Balloon Glow. The race marked its twenty-fifth anniversary with a special celebration in 1997. Because of reconstruction work at its usual venue on the Gateway Arch grounds, Fair St. Louis came to the park from downtown in 2015 and easily accommodated some one hundred thousand people for the spectacular fireworks display.

Another addition to the park, announced in 2001, was the Norman K. Probstein Golf Clubhouse, the product of a $2 million gift to Forest Park Forever from hotelier Norman

Top left, Balloon Glow, September 16, 2005. *Right,* Great Forest Park Balloon Race Glow in Central Field, September 9, 2013. *Bottom left,* fireworks at the finale of the St. Louis Symphony's concert in Forest Park, September 17, 2013

Forest Park scenes (*left to right*): the World's Fair Pavilion, a bridge with Washington University in the distance, Kennedy Forest, and a suspension bridge

Probstein, nephew of Sam Koplar and cousin of Harold Koplar of the Chase Park Plaza. Probstein had also built the 128-room Bel Air West (later the Best Western Inn at the Park) on Lindell.

Also in 2001 came the first production of the new Shakespeare Festival held in a natural amphitheater, later dubbed "Shakespeare Glen," in Forest Park. R. Crosby Kemper III, then a St. Louisan, founded the event. "Wherefore art thou, my Romeo?" asked Juliet in a well-attended series of June performances of *Romeo and Juliet*. Since then, the popular festival has staged productions of other Shakespeare plays, such as *Much Ado about Nothing*,

Richard III, *A Midsummer Night's Dream*, and *Twelfth Night*.

In 2007, controversy erupted over a 9.4-acre patch of parkland, detached from the main park area by Kingshighway and already leased to Barnes-Jewish Hospital, which had built tennis and racquetball courts above ground and a parking lot below. The hospital agreed to pay $2 million for a long-term lease, and Forest Park Forever endorsed the plan; the city approved it in March. But in April, Prop P—a charter amendment to require voter approval before city parkland could be "sold, leased, given away or otherwise disposed of"—won at the polls, thanks to the efforts of Citizens to Protect Forest Park.

Over the years, all the cultural attractions in the park had been growing and improving. In 1991, the Saint Louis Science Center opened on Oakland Avenue after a $34 million construction project that included a bridge to the James S. McDonnell Planetarium and a five-story OmniMax Theater. Since then, it has added an Exploradome in 1997 and Boeing Hall in 2011. The Jewel Box fended off a 1991 budgetary threat to its existence and in 2002 had a $3.5 million renovation. In 1994, the Muny founded its popular Muny Kids group. In 2000, the Missouri History Museum added a major piece to its Lindell building: the Emerson Center, designed by HOK, which more than tripled its space. The Saint Louis Art Museum began construction in 2009 on a long-hoped-for $130 million expansion. The Saint Louis Zoo opened many new attractions, including the new River's Edge in 2002, Penguin & Puffin Coast in 2003, as well as the Mary Ann Lee Conservation Carousel, Sea Lion Sound in 2012, and the $16 million Polar Bear Point in 2016. The Dennis and Judith Jones Visitor and Education Center underwent a $4 million renovation, and the World's Fair Pavilion had a $1.1 million restoration in the early twenty-first century.

In the 1980s, the Saint Louis Ambassadors, a civic group, renovated the historic Cabanne House, built in

The vacant Cabanne House before renovation by the Saint Louis Ambassadors, 1986

1876 at 5300 Lindell near the entrance to Forest Park. Until the group mounted its fundraising effort, the building was at risk of demolition. It had been damaged by a 1966 fire and was vacant after being used for years by city agencies. The Ambassadors moved their offices to the building and rent it for events.

Admission to many of these attractions was free thanks to the Metropolitan Zoological Park and Museum District, established by city and county voters in 1972 with three institutions: the art museum, the zoo, and the science center. The Missouri Botanical Garden was added to the group in 1983 and the history museum in 1987, though voters refused to allow a proposed tax increase rate for the science center in 1989.

CHANGING OF THE GUARD

From the 1980s through 2016, many longtime businesses moved, changed hands, or vanished. A 1980 tidbit in Joe Pollack's *Post-Dispatch* column titled "Hello Euclid, So Long Wales," announced the opening of Dressel's, a pub located at 419 North Euclid in the space formerly occupied by Katmandu. Owner Jon Dressel, who had been teaching in Wales, had also partnered with Jack Brangle to operate Llywelyn's Pub at 4747 McPherson, which served Welsh dishes. Llywelyn's came under new ownership in 1997 and then broadened its size and menu.

A building that had generated many complaints over the years from residents disappeared in the late 1990s: the white, circular building at 4560 West Pine

Top, **Duff's, 2011;** *bottom,* **Llywelyn's Pub, undated**

that had once housed the West Pine Tower Nursing Home, previously the Carlson Tower Geriatric Center and the Regency Nursing Inn. The fifteen-story tower was replaced with townhouses.

In 2011, the Webster-Kirkwood Times Inc., under President Dwight Bitikofer, purchased the *West End Word,* which then had a circulation of around twenty thousand. After some forty years in the area, Rothschild's Antiques, a longtime occupant of 398 North Euclid, moved out of the neighborhood in 2012, and the Mexican restaurant Gringo took its place. In 2013, Duff's—a "Class of 72" restaurant—served its last meals, as co-owners Karen Duffy and Tim Kirby retired. Big Sleep Books, which had sold mysteries for twenty-seven years, closed in 2015, and co-owner Helen Simpson died in the same year. In 2016, Herbie's Vintage 72 also moved to Clayton, taking the spot formerly occupied by Cardwell's.

All photos, **people dining in the Central West End, 2011**

NEW DEVELOPMENTS

Over time, dozens of real estate firms and brokers began offering homes for sale in the Central West End, their ads filling pages in the *West End Word*. New projects also sprang up in the area. By 1988, the Union-Sarah Economic Development Corporation "had stimulated more than $55 million in residential and commercial developments in one of the previously most desolate parts of the neighborhood," wrote Swanstrom and Webber in their "Rebound Neighborhoods" report. McCormack Baron Salazar, a company that became "a national leader in mixed-income housing developments, also developed housing in the CWE," they said, including the successful Westminster Place project at Westminster, Olive, and McPherson. Builder Jerry King, who formerly headed WUMCRC, mounted projects in the neighborhood. In 2000, the Third Eye Investment and Development Corporation planned to build sixteen new houses in the 4200 block of Delmar between Pendleton and Whittier.

In 2002, Conrad Properties acquired a large apartment complex at Forest Park and Euclid, owned by Paraquad since 1977, for more than $2 million. Paraquad had relinquished the building at the request of HUD, which wished to relocate its disabled residents rather than rehab the facility. The 82-unit Boulevard Apartments was demolished, and Metro

Chouteau Condominiums, mid-1980s

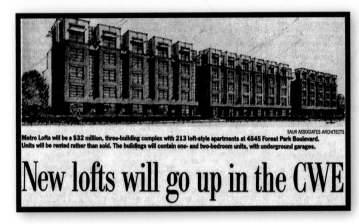

Metro Lofts will be a $32 million, three-building complex with 213 loft-style apartments at 4545 Forest Park Boulevard. Units will be rented rather than sold. The buildings will contain one- and two-bedroom units, with underground garages.

SAUR ASSOCIATES ARCHITECTS

New lofts will go up in the CWE

Ad for the new Metro Lofts

Plans for a new Whole Foods Market and City Walk Apartments, 2013

Lofts with 213 loft-style rental apartments and underground garages replaced it at a cost of $32 million. Barbara Geisman, the city's deputy mayor for development, said that what was planned on Forest Park Boulevard "will be the first apartment complex of its kind in the city."

The hoped-for redevelopment on Maryland Plaza was finally completed in 2007 when Ted Koplar and his son Sam eliminated the controversial cobblestones, installed a new fountain, rehabilitated retail and office space, attracted a restaurant, and restored three buildings. In 2012, a $12 million renovation of the Chase Apartments—now the York House—was also finished.

In 2016, Whole Foods Market opened a new 28,480-square-foot store at 4577 West Pine and Euclid, the chain's third location in the area. The store occupied the first floor of the $75 million City Walk, a new seven-story, 176-apartment building at 4577 West Pine. That site was previously occupied by the eleven-story Doctors' Building, 100 North Euclid, that housed the offices of Reproductive Health Services, then Missouri's busiest abortion clinic, which made it the target of frequent anti-abortion protests.

"Our campus today is growing. We are attracting faculty and students from all over the world, and patients are coming to us in increasing numbers. It is just a wonderful success story for St. Louis. And if you look at the medical center's location on Kingshighway: to our south is Forest Park Southeast, to our east is the Cortex district, and to our north is the Central West End. All three areas have gone through periods of revitalization, growth, and renewal.

"I think when people like Bill Danforth, John McDonnell, and John Dubinsky saw the influence that the medical center had on the Central West End, they looked east and saw the opportunity for a biotech district that would bring high technology and good-paying jobs to St. Louis. Then they looked south and saw Forest Park Southeast, both the impact that poverty and crime had had on that neighborhood and the need to revitalize its housing stock and commercial district. That remarkable vision has resulted in enormous progress.

"Look at the medical center and its component parts—that aggregation of medical oomph and higher education oomph—and its commitment to the city of St. Louis and to revitalized city neighborhoods. That is a powerful example of what we can accomplish when we combine the public sector and private sector; the not-for-profit, for-profit, and entrepreneurial sectors. When they all come together, good things can happen."

—Steven Lipstein,
CEO of BJC HealthCare

Top, students on the Washington University Medical School campus, 2015. *Bottom,* aerial view of Danforth Campus, facing east, 2010.

THE IMPACT OF WUMCRC

Altogether, the Central West End was flourishing. Nearby, the Washington University Medical Center was growing with more than twenty thousand people working there daily. From a neighborhood in crisis, the area had emerged as a diverse, stable place with fourteen thousand residents, exciting new businesses, and a mix of historic buildings and new development.

Would it all have happened without the decision of the Washington University Medical Center to stand its ground, stay in the neighborhood, and improve its surroundings? "That decision may be one of the five most important decisions ever made in terms of the history of the city of St. Louis," said Jerry King. "Because if the Washington University Medical Center had left the city of St. Louis, can you imagine what the city of St. Louis would be like? I mean it's hard to imagine. The impact would have been huge."

Richard Ward agreed. "I don't think the Central West End would have achieved anywhere near the success it has achieved. It would not have become a dump; I think market forces would gradually have turned more positive, and better things would have happened. But that would have been a decade slower, and there would be a lot more loss. Without the strength the medical center has given it, it would certainly not have been as successful as it has been."

VENTURE CAFÉ

The Venture Café, a place to gather and share ideas in the Cortex Innovation District

"NO END IN SIGHT"

A Foundation for Future Success

◦◦~◦◦

"The redevelopment of the Central West End is ongoing. While there was arguably a starting point in the story when the Washington University Medical Center drew a line in the sand, there is no end in sight."

—Richard Roloff,
real estate developer and
first head of WUMCRC

BUCKINGHAM HOTEL

Proposed New Buckingham Hotel, King's Highway and West Pine Boulevard, to Cost $1,500,000, *St. Louis Post-Dispatch*, **January 11, 1903**

The predecessor of the proposed "One Hundred" building was also a fashionable building in its day. In January 1903, developers announced plans to build the "strictly first-class" Buckingham Hotel on that site. The ten-story building would have 537 guest rooms, plus a "magnificent palm garden and ballroom finished in the Renaissance style of architecture." Further, "all the corridors will be finished in mosaic and imported marble." The cost? A breathtaking $1.5 million.

That spring, the builders had trouble securing financing, but in the end they got enough to build a seven-story hotel for $500,000. "The project had been regarded as dead," said one newspaper story, "but like Banquo's ghost, it would not [stay] down." But at 450 rooms (300 with bath), it was still swanky enough that Secretary of State John Hay checked in when he visited the World's Fair. The hotel also had a prized ventilating system that suggested its early advertising slogan, "the coolest place in the city."

Over the years, many events—balls and dinner dances, luncheons and card parties—took place there. Along the way, the hotel built an annex at 4958 West Pine to handle the overflow. In 1920, its residents appealed to authorities to stop a wealthy grain dealer next door from keeping chickens, pigeons, ducks, and dogs at his home. "Life in the Annex, once well-ordered and harmonious," said a newspaper account, "now is punctuated . . . with cackling, crowing, barking and quacking."

Buckingham Hotel Annex after fire, 1930

More serious was a December 1927 fire at the annex that killed seven residents. The hotel was not damaged, but after the Chase Hotel went up, it lost its panache. Soon it became the Kings-Way. Then in 1931, disaster struck again when the safe at the hotel was looted and $15,000 worth of residents' jewelry disappeared. In

Hotel Ambassador being razed in 1973

1957, new owners acquired the Kings-Way and redeveloped it as the Ambassador, with such additions as a glassed-in roof terrace. In 1960, fire broke out, and three guests were taken to the hospital. In 1964, a group headed by Harold Koplar bought it. Then in 1971, another fire killed four, and in 1973 the historic building was demolished, creating a vacant lot.

T he revitalization of the Central West End was successful—so successful, in fact, that it spawned a host of other projects. Within the neighborhood, it laid the groundwork for innovative development ideas, such as a 36-story apartment tower planned for a parking lot at Kingshighway and Lindell.

The $130 million, 305-unit project—officially named "One Hundred" but nicknamed "Stacked Cups" or "Magazine Rack" for its dramatic, contemporary design featuring an angled-glass facade—had a hoped-for completion date of 2019.

Proposed 36-story apartment tower, 2016

While William Peck was dean of the Washington University School of Medicine from 1988 to 2003, he said, "the Forest Park Southeast area began to loom as a real threat to us because it was so deteriorated, and it was right across the bridge. I pushed hard for its redevelopment, and [physician] Jerry Flance was my representative in that process; the redevelopment corporation provided oversight. [Developer] Richard Baron was unbelievable, and we couldn't have done it without him. We transformed the area."

Intended as a nine-year effort, the WUMCRC effort—now a partnership between the School of Medicine and BJC HealthCare—is continuing more than forty years later under director Brian Phillips. Today, its goals include the strengthening of Forest Park Southeast and the Central West End in such areas as housing, social service initiatives, and security. WUMCRC has partnered with the Central West End, for example, in supporting the Neighborhood Security Initiative (447 North Euclid), established in 2007 to work with local police on crime prevention and quick response times. Partners in this work are the Special Business Districts, established by WUMCRC and the Central West End Association, which provide funding for neighborhood security efforts that include increased patrolling by off-duty officers.

Brookings Hall at Washington University

LAYING THE GROUNDWORK FOR NEW VENTURES

Washington University is also a lead partner in a breathtaking new venture: the Cortex Innovation Community, located east of the medical center adjacent to the Central West End. That project was one outgrowth of a startling realization. In the late 1990s, three Washington University engineering faculty members, including Jerome Cox, developed a switch for getting information quickly on and off the Internet. For two years they tried and failed to attract funding to start a company locally, but in San Francisco they got the help they needed. "In less than a year, the company was established and sold for $350 million," says William Danforth. "All the jobs and most of the money went to the West Coast. The lesson—that St. Louis must develop its own enterprises rather than just export good ideas—was shared with civic and institutional partners."

They needed to prevent such losses in the future, especially since St. Louis was likely to produce further innovations in life sciences, biomedicine, and agriculture. So in 2000, the Danforth Foundation and Civic Progress provided funding to the Regional

Mark Wrighton

Left to right, **Donn Rubin, William Danforth, Roger Beachy**

Washington University students in springtime

Left, **The Brookings arch into the main quadrangle**

Commerce and Growth Association (RCGA), so they could bring in an Ohio-based research-and-development firm, the Battelle Memorial Institute, to study the problem. Their team, which met with many community groups and leaders, developed a plan that "catalyzed a community consensus that the life sciences were a tremendous economic opportunity for St. Louis, and people had not recognized that before," says Donn Rubin, who today is president and CEO of BioSTL, an organization dedicated to advancing the life sciences in St. Louis through an array of programs, from developing entrepreneurs and physical infrastructure to building and funding biotech start-ups.

Only months later, at the beginning of 2001, Rubin—who had previously led projects for former senator John Danforth's civic improvement effort, St. Louis 2004—was hired to become executive director of a predecessor to BioSTL: the Coalition for Plant and Life Sciences, representing a range of civic and educational institutions. They formed three key committees: capital, headed first by Robert Virgil and then by John McDonnell; federal policy, by physician Virginia Weldon; and facilities, the largest of all, headed by newly retired banker

John Dubinsky

Left and above, **two views of the Donald Danforth Plant Science Center**

Steven Lipstein

John Dubinsky. "One day, Bill Danforth called and said he'd like to come see me, which, of course, was an honor," recalled Dubinsky. "Then Bill said, 'How would you like to lead the effort to try to figure out how we are going to put facilities in St. Louis to support the beginnings and growth of a biotechnology industry?' I asked, 'Well, what do you really want me to do?' And he said, 'John, if I knew what to do, I would do it myself.'"

Just then, Danforth and Rubin learned that several new firms, including RiverVest Venture Partners and Prolog Ventures, could not raise a fund here. So Washington University, the Danforth Foundation, and the McDonnell family each committed $40 million to jump-start St. Louis venture capital funds in a coordinated way. RiverVest got off the ground with a $21 million collective investment and Prolog with $15 million. Also in 2001 came another seminal scientific effort in St. Louis, spearheaded by William Danforth: the construction of the original Donald Danforth Plant Science Center building on its Creve Coeur campus. This nonprofit center, founded in 1998, focused on a three-part mission: feeding the hungry, preserving the environment, and building the economy of the region.

BOSTON TRIP SPARKS PROGRESS

All three committees of the Coalition for Plant and Life Sciences began brainstorming and planning. "But there was no silver bullet," adds Danforth. "We had learned from the Battelle Institute that to be successful in developing new companies our community needed supporting strengths in education, science, start-up creation, investments, real estate, legal and accounting skills, political understanding, and public policies."

An RCGA-sponsored leadership trip in 2001 cemented this lesson. That year, the RCGA took a group to Boston, where they heard the head of real estate for MIT talk about the school's substantial investment—15 percent of its endowment—in their Cambridge neighborhood of Kendall Square. In a five-year process, they had revitalized one square mile of space as a vibrant mixed-use development with an explosion of biotechnology and IT companies, plus space for new housing, restaurants, shopping, and recreation. Rubin, Danforth, and Dubinsky were on the trip, "and we said to each other, 'if they can do it, Washington University ought to be able to do it too.' But we also knew that the university shouldn't be doing it alone; there should be partners in this project," recalls Rubin.

The Boston trip soon became the catalyst for at least two advances in St. Louis, and one was a new venture capital fund. Danforth renewed an acquaintance with Peter Brooke, founder and CEO emeritus of Advent International, a global private equity firm. Brooke and his son, John, started a venture fund in St. Louis, Vectis, whose annual meetings acquainted out-of-town investors with promising local scientific projects.

An even more momentous result of the trip was a strengthened determination to found a Cambridge-style innovation district in St. Louis. As soon as the group came back, Danforth convened a landmark breakfast meeting with several key players—the leaders from Washington University, BJC HealthCare, the University of Missouri–St. Louis, Saint Louis University, and the Missouri Botanical Garden, along with the city of St. Louis and the Regional Commerce and Growth Association—to talk about the vision and funding for such a project. Universally, there was enthusiasm for the idea, and when they polled people around the table to ask what they would give, the total was an astonishing $150,000 in seed money, more than they had hoped. So the planning moved briskly forward.

"I became involved in Cortex very soon after I was elected mayor. In 2002, I was part of the big kickoff meeting, talking about the idea of creating an innovation district. These were leaders of major institutions but also strong civic leaders and regional advocates. They were all saying that they wanted to grow their businesses, and they also wanted to do all they could for the future of the region to make it an exciting place and build an environment for what they saw as the new economy.

"My first thought was: 'Wow, this is great: all these great minds pulling together not only to put together a vision, but also to say we're going to make this happen.' It was very, very exciting. Very, very exciting. Too often, we find ourselves splitting off in different ways. This was a meeting I walked away from thinking, 'We can really accomplish great things if we can harness this energy.' It was a very positive moment for me as mayor.

"Since then, Cortex has gotten a lot of attention around the nation and even the world. I went to one mayor's meeting where there was a session showcasing a few cities where there are really successful innovation districts. One of those cities was St. Louis. The presenter said: 'If any of you mayors want to start an innovation district from scratch, go to St. Louis.' I'm sitting there, and mayors are turning to me and thinking: 'Oh, that's what is going on in St. Louis.' That made me very proud."

—Former mayor Francis Slay

"The improvement around the university must continue. We are an institution that is growing. We see enormous opportunity in the era ahead, and we are looking forward to working with St. Louis, its communities, and its people. We believe that by having strong communities we will be stronger.

"MIT is a great institution, but the surrounding area hasn't always been so great. In fact, when I joined the MIT faculty in 1972, Kendall Square was a difficult part of Cambridge. Today, it is vibrant, and in that area is the Cambridge Innovation Center. In a single building, they have something like four hundred start-up companies.

We encouraged them to come out for a visit to learn about what we are trying to do, and they selected Cortex for their first innovation center outside Cambridge.

"Our region will thrive in the future if we're able to attract talented young people, and they want to be in urban environments. They want to be part of new enterprises. Cortex is attracting new people to the community and assisting in retaining those who come to St. Louis for their university education. These young people are our uture."

—Mark Wrighton,
Chancellor of Washington University

Aerial view of the Cortex redevelopment project in its early stages

Blanche Touhill

CORTEX GETS OFF THE GROUND

Still, the major investment in this effort was yet to come. Each institution that had given seed money had to decide how much it could allocate to actually mount the project. While the Missouri Botanical Garden was unable to contribute, Washington University committed $15 million; Saint Louis University and BJC each gave $5 million. UMSL, under Chancellor Blanche Touhill, promised $4 million, which they would somehow trim from their operating budget.

Where would this new urban innovation center be located? The Coalition for Plant and Life Sciences had identified two neighborhoods as prospects: Creve Coeur, near the new Danforth Plant Science Center; and a 200-acre site in midtown St. Louis. The planners decided that this new innovation district, like the MIT development, would be built between the Washington University Medical Center on the west and Saint Louis University on the east. But another aspect of this location, its proximity to the revitalized Central West End, was also a crucial point in its favor, because it would make this site appealing to young workers. "The really blighted parts of the neighborhood had been cleared out, so it didn't feel like we were drowning in urban blight," says John Dubinsky, who went on to serve as Cortex's first CEO and then its first board chairman. "We decided that the Redevelopment Corporation had created an environment we could build on and make better."

"Cortex was a creature of the early twenty-first century, around 2002, when Bill Danforth and John Dubinsky came to me to discuss their idea of creating a district for the development of the life sciences. This idea actually went back to the 1980s with Technopolis, the same kind of concept: we were going to create a technology quarter in our city. It was a nice idea, but it sat on a shelf somewhere. Then Bill Danforth and John Dubinsky picked up the pieces.

"For this new organization, we didn't want to use the same name. So one Saturday afternoon I was in my office sitting at my computer, trying to come up with a name. I didn't want to call it 'Newco'; lawyers always call new companies 'Newco.' Then I thought: 'Cortex—the brain.' It was an acronym, but for words I hadn't put together yet. So I said, 'well what goes with Cortex? Center of Research, Technology and Entrepreneurial Expertise. That was a mouthful but it fit. So we took that on and actually used it, though we changed the 'e' to 'exchange.' Years later, I remember saying at one or more board meetings that we'd use it for a time and then finally come up with a name. But the name has stuck, and it's still 'Cortex.'"

—Harvey Harris,
attorney and civic leader involved in the creation of Cortex

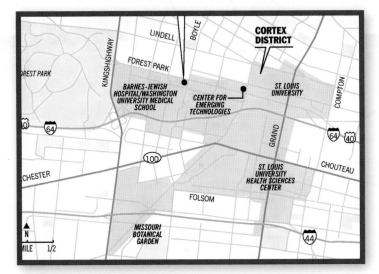

St. Louis Post-Dispatch map of the Cortex District in relation to the Central West End and surrounding universities, 2004

Medical research hub will expand

CORTEX project will double size of its Central West End campus.

BY TIM LOGAN
tlogan@post-dispatch.com > 314-340-8291

The city's biggest science park is about to get bigger.

CORTEX is poised to start construction next spring on a $140 million expansion that will nearly double the size of its campus in the Central West End, said president Dennis Lower.

It plans to rehab two industrial buildings and put up a 150,000 square foot new building, with most of the space already committed to BJC Healthcare and Wexford Science and Technology — a developer of science labs. When done in late 2013, CORTEX expects the 19-acre site to house 1,600 jobs.

It is Phase Two of the massive CORTEX redevelopment, a nonprofit joint venture by area universities, BJC and the Missouri Botanical Garden that aims to turn about 240 acres of small factories and warehouses east of Washington University Medical Center into a thriving hub for medical research. The first phase, which included a lab building on Forest Park Parkway and the headquarters of plant science firm Solae Corp., is just about full, Lower said.

"We're at 97 percent occupancy," he said. "We need space."

St. Louis Post-Dispatch,
November 11, 2001

Dubinsky, with help from Lewis Levey and Harvey Harris, oversaw construction of the first two buildings. Meanwhile, Rubin obtained $12 million in state tax credits from Governor Robert Holden's administration, with matching contributions from local corporations and foundations, which helped assemble forty acres within the planned district. They attracted new businesses and embarked on some mixed-use development, such as the Central West End Lofts. After Dubinsky stepped down, Richard Roloff took over for a time, securing as a tenant in the Cortex 1 building the BioGenerator: a nonprofit start-up creator and seed fund established in 2002 by the Coalition for Plant and Life Sciences, with funding largely supplied by John McDonnell, who today chairs the BioSTL board. Roloff also initiated a fruitful relationship with developer Wexford Science & Technology, which built the Bio-Research & Development Growth Park near the Danforth Plant Science Center before shifting over to develop property at Cortex.

By 2010, they were ready for a permanent executive to manage Cortex. UMSL chancellor Thomas George chaired the search, assisted by Rubin, and the choice fell to Dennis Lower, who had previously worked on the development of research parks in Louisiana and New Jersey. Since then, Cortex has grown substantially. In 2009, McDonnell and

The Venture Café at
Cortex, December 2016

Rubin arranged the merger into Cortex of the Center for Emerging Technologies, a nearby innovation center founded in 1998, which had helped launch such ventures as Orion Genomics and Metaphase. Another addition is the Cambridge Innovation Center (CIC), which opened in November 2016 in an old telephone factory on Duncan Avenue.

CORTEX FLOURISHES

Today, Cortex has some 1.7 million square feet of space under construction, and it is home to more than 250 bioscience, information technology, and engineering companies representing more than four thousand jobs. Some businesses, such as Orion or iSelect, are start-ups; others, such as Boeing with its idea generator Ventures, Dupont and Bunge with their subsidiary Solae, BJC HealthCare, or Express Scripts, are pieces of large companies. At weekly sessions in the Venture Café, located in the @4240 building, entrepreneurs compare ideas and socialize. In 2016, RiverVest moved to Cortex with an office at BioGenerator; so did Square, a mobile-payment company. AAIPharma Services Corporation/Cambridge Major Laboratories Inc. announced plans to relocate its business, previously on South Lindbergh Blvd., to a $10.7 million analytical testing facility in the brand-new 4260 building at Boyle and Forest Park.

Late in 2016, Cortex previewed its Phase III expansion, to include a boutique hotel by Starwood, a five-story technology and lab building, an innovation

AREA OF THE PLANNED IKEA DEVELOPMENT

Dennis Lower *left,* president and CEO of Cortex, and Reed Lyons, real estate manager for Ikea St. Louis, *St. Louis Post-Dispatch* June 29, 2014

St. Louis Post-Dispatch map of the new Ikea store in relation to nearby buildings, June 29, 2014

hall, and a parking garage. In 2018, it will also have its own Boyle Avenue MetroLink light-rail station and a connection to the Great Rivers Greenway Trail System. Eventually, Cortex hopes to grow to $2.3 billion in construction, with 4.5 million square feet of mixed-used development, 450 companies, and 13,000 jobs.

Another coup for Cortex was attracting the popular Swedish home furnishings retailer Ikea to a 21-acre piece of its site. Its 300,000-square-foot store, which opened late in 2015, represents some $100 million in investment by Ikea—an infusion of funds for Cortex and a tax boon for the city. The Lawrence Group announced plans to

redevelop the empty Federal-Mogul foundry in the 3700 block of Forest Park Avenue as City Foundry. The first phase of the project, to be finished within two years, includes a food hall, retail space, and offices. A second phase could mean construction of a 24-story apartment building and office buildings, all for around $340 million.

"A GREAT SUCCESS STORY"

Despite all the exciting news, more remains to be accomplished in the Central West End and just across its borders. Violent crime occasionally troubles the neighborhood. In 2016, there were six homicides in

"Square and Cortex were a wonderful marriage. When Square was looking for an expansion location, I suggested St. Louis, and we considered a lot of areas around the city. But Cortex has a fantastic vibe. First of all, it has these beautiful old buildings, it has this great connectivity to the rest of the city, and it also has enough space available to play with. The space we are in today, twelve months ago, used to be a garage. So we had a blank canvas for creating this fantastic space. So Square coming to Cortex was a combination of the great vibe they have created at Cortex and a canvas we could draw on."

—Jim McKelvey,
cofounder of Third Degree Glass,
cofounder of Square,
and founder of LaunchCode to train people for programming jobs

Art Hill and the Grand Basin in Forest Park

Central West End residents gather in cafés.

the area, including a taxi driver and a resident. Sheena Greitens, wife of Governor Eric Greitens and a Central West End resident, was robbed at gunpoint outside a café near Saint Louis University. Another risk for the future is gentrification, said Todd Swanstrom, the University of Missouri–St. Louis public policy expert. "Right now, I don't think it is a serious threat because rents are still relatively affordable, and there are affordable units available through subsidies. But as the area continues to succeed, at a certain point rents could take off, and you create a neighborhood that is no longer exciting and edgy with a bunch of wealthy professionals—and artists can't afford to live there anymore."

More progress also needs to happen north of Delmar. "It's not all as peachy as it looks to those of us on the south side of Delmar, the great divide," said journalist Robert Duffy. "North of Delmar, there are laudable efforts and parts that have maintained themselves beautifully, but there are also elements of the Wild West. We need to figure out ways to change that situation: not to create nice, white, middle-class neighborhoods, but a decent place for anyone who chooses to live there. We made some progress and did some things that are durable—and we did it with very little money—but we're not done."

Local scenes (*left to right*): **the Delmar Loop, a Forest Park walking trail, the new Citizen Park building on Lindell, and the Boathouse in Forest Park**

Yet the news is overwhelmingly positive. In their report, authors Swanstrom and Webber named the Central West End as one of the area's most successful "Rebound Neighborhoods." "From 2000 to the present," they wrote, "the CWE has undoubtedly become one of the most desirable and affluent urban neighborhoods in the St. Louis region. Housing prices in the neighborhood have increased substantially, with homes that sold for under $30,000 in the early 1970s now costing over $500,000, even as the area has maintained racial and economic diversity." The racial diversity has actually increased, they added. "It is among the most diverse neighborhoods in the region, with African American, white, Asian, and some Hispanic. And I think diversity is an asset for the area."

Altogether, the Central West End has come full circle: from its origins in wealth and privilege, through its downhill slide, to its period of gradual rebirth, and now to its robust new life. It's a story of courage shown by committed citizens, neighborhood groups, churches, politicians, and the Washington University Medical Center. It's also a story of redemption, showing that when well-intentioned people come together in an important cause they can prevail. But the role of the medical center was key. Without its intervention, says radiologist Ronald Evens, "I don't think there was anybody else in the city who had the gumption to do it. The concerns about our northern and eastern flank would have been there. I think it would have been horrible." But the efforts of the medical center in cooperation with residents and

others, he adds, "not only stopped out-flight but made the Central West End one of the best areas in town. I mean, it's a great success story."

And this success has generated a ripple effect, with rings of further success swirling outward. "The Central West End," says Will Ross, area resident and Washington University School of Medicine physician, acts as "a catalyst for the growth of progressive thought, and that brings in people who are looking for creativity, innovation, and wonderful opportunities. I drive around and see that same thing happening in University City and Forest Park Southeast; there is no reason why it can't happen north of Delmar. Now people are looking to the university as a main driver: 'We believe you now, we've seen what you've done.

And we want you to be our neighbor in this effort to drive this expansion, this phenomenal dynamism that comes from having all these cultures interact.' That's how great communities are created."

"I hope that St. Louisans and people from surrounding areas will continue to cooperate to improve their home region with concern for the whole instead of just their own piece of turf," adds William Danforth. "If so, I foresee a great future for us all." ❧

ACKNOWLEDGMENTS

Above all, I would like to express my thanks to Dr. William H. Danforth, former chancellor of Washington University, who had a vision for this effort: to tell the story of the Central West End and its rich history, and to capture the seminal role of the Washington University Medical Center in its rebirth. I am also grateful to former St. Louis mayor Francis Slay, who provided a foreword for the book.

Special gratitude also goes to Cortex pioneer John Dubinsky for his help with this book and the other piece of this project: the two-part documentary on the Central West End and Cortex. That documentary was created by the Nine Network under the able leadership of Jack Galmiche. The network's wonderfully creative producer/director, Patrick Murphy, conducted dozens of interviews and made these two films with lavish care just before his retirement. My thanks to him and his talented film crew, headed by Laurent Torno III, for allowing me to take part in many interviews and for showing such collegiality and generosity throughout.

The Missouri History Museum and its president Dr. Frances Levine have also been generous partners, supplying advice, research assistance, and dozens of images through their terrific archivists: Jaime Bourassa, Dennis Northcott, and Molly Kodner. It would also have been impossible to assemble the many thousands of details and hundreds of images without the assistance of several wonderful Washington University graduate students and part-time faculty. Jon Lee was extraordinarily helpful in gathering books, articles, and data. Jen Arch was a wonder in transcribing the interviews. Kelly Oman was the excellent photo editor, who patiently and meticulously assembled countless images; she also constructed the index. Without her, the book would not have been possible.

A warm thank you to Reedy Press, which published this book with help from the designer, Richard Roden; the fine copyeditor, and excellent printer. Working with Josh Stevens and Barbara Northcott has been a great pleasure, and I am very grateful for their talents.

My sincere appreciation goes to all those, too numerous to list here, who participated in interviews and contributed information. On the photo side, I owe special gratitude to Cabanne Howard from the World Chess Hall of Fame; Anne McAlpin of the Mary Institute Archives; Brian Holder and Patrick Murphy of the Nine Network; the staff at the Saint Louis Zoo, Forest Park Forever, the Central West End Association, and the *West End Word*; Theresa Howard of the Washington University School of Medicine; Joe Angeles of Washington University; Brian Phillips of the Washington University Medical Center Redevelopment Corporation; Sue Rehkopf of the Episcopal Diocese of Missouri; Todd Swanstrom and Jenny Connelly-Bower of UMSL; the Rev. Donald Cochran of Second Presbyterian Church; and Shelley Hagen, curator, Wells Fargo Enterprise Marketing. Thanks also to the *Post-Dispatch* for its many wonderful newspaper images.

Along with the Missouri History Museum, other archives helped with information, and I owe thanks to many archivists and librarians, including Stephen Logsdon, Philip Skroska, and Caitlin Crane of the Becker Archives at the Washington University School of Medicine; Charles Brown at the St. Louis Mercantile Library; and Sonya Rooney and Miranda Rectenwald at Washington University. Mary Ann Noel and Gayle Derouin deserve thanks for helping with this project and reading the manuscript.

A BIBLIOGRAPHIC NOTE

Among my key resources in writing this book were the newspaper and magazine archives of the periodicals that have covered St. Louis, principally the St. Louis Post-Dispatch. I have consulted many others as well, among them the *St. Louis Globe-Democrat*, the *West End Word*, *St. Louis Magazine*, the *St. Louis Star*, the *St. Louis Business Journal*, and the *St. Louis Republic*. Publications of the Washington University Medical Center—*Outlook Magazine*, the *Barnes Hospital Bulletin*, and 216 (Jewish Hospital)—also contained helpful information.

I was grateful for professional articles, including an important report written by Todd Swanstrom and Hank Webber: "Rebound Neighborhoods in Older Industrial Cities: The Story of St. Louis" (2014). Richard Ward was kind enough to supply me with articles in professional publications that he had written on the revitalization efforts.

Let me add that I consulted many publications for the "official" boundaries of the Central West End—but various people and resources treat that differently, so I adopted a definition that seemed sensible.

Since these articles and publications are usually referenced in the text, I have not cited them in footnote form but trust that contextual references will be sufficient.

I combed through many Central West End–related books, primarily:

St. Louis Lost: Uncovering the City's Architectural Treasures, Mary Bartley (1994)

The Days and Nights of the Central West End, Suzanne Goell (1992 edition)

Terrace Tales: A Contemporary History of Washington Terrace, Street of Mansions, Jeff Tallent (1992)

Westmoreland and Portland Places: The History and Architecture of America's Premier Private Streets, 1888–1988, Julius K. Hunter (1988)

Central West End, Albert Montesi and Richard Deposki (2000)

St. Louis: Historic Churches and Synagogues, Mary M. Stiritz (1998)

Architecture of the Private Streets of St. Louis: The Architects and the Houses They Designed, Charles Savage (1987)

Kingsbury Place: The First Two Hundred Years, Julius K. Hunter (1982)

Forest Park, Caroline Loughlin and Catherine Anderson (1986)

Literary St. Louis: A Guide, Lorin Cuoco (2000)

History of St. Louis Neighborhoods, Norbury Wayman (1978)

Pictorial St. Louis: The Great Metropolis of the Mississippi Valley, Richard Compton & Camille Dry (1876)

The Book of St. Louisans: A Biographical Dictionary of the Leading Living Men of the City of St. Louis, Albert Nelson Marquis (1912)

I also drew from material I had gathered for two books of my own:

Beginning a Great Work, Washington University in St. Louis, 1853–2003 (2003)

Meet Me in the Lobby: The Story of Harold Koplar and the Chase Park Plaza (2005)

INDEX

PHOTO CREDITS

Becker Medical Archives, Washington University School of Medicine: *IV, 4 (right), 7 (top), 10, 11 (middle, right top, right bottom), 18 (bottom), 22 (right), 26 (top right), 47, 68, 71 (left), 75 (top), 77 (bottom left, bottom right), 78, 79 (both), 80 (both), 81, 83, 84 (all), 85 (both), 87 (top, middle, bottom right), 120 (top), 121 (top left, bottom), 142 (top), 161 (top), 162 (both), 163 (both), 166 (top), 169 (all), 170, 175 (bottom left, bottom right), 201, 213 (both), 215 (both), 216, 222, 225 (all), 226 (left), 228, 230, 231 (all), 232, 233, 236, 237, 238, 243 (bottom), 244 (bottom), 245 (both), 247 (all), 248 (both), 251, 276 (both)*

Missouri History Museum: *Front cover (top left, bottom right and left), X, 2 (all), 3 (right), 11 (left), 12, 13 (both), 15, 16, 17, 20, 21 (both), 22 (left), 24 (left), 26 (left), 27 (all), 28 (both), 30, 31, 32 (all), 33 (both), 34 (both), 35, 36 (top), 37, 38, 39 (both), 41 (both), 42, 43, 44, 45, 46, 48, 49 (both), 50 (both), 51, 52 (all), 53 (both), 54 (bottom), 55 (middle, bottom), 56, 57 (all), 58 (all), 59, 60 (top), 61, 62 (left), 64, 65 (all), 66, 70 (both), 71 (right), 77 (top), 86 (left, top right), 87 (bottom left, bottom middle), 89 (top), 90, 91 (all), 96, 97 (top), 98 (both), 99 (left), 102, 104 (top), 105 (top), 106 (right), 107 (top, bottom), 108 (both), 109, 110, 111 (both), 112 (both), 113, 114 (top), 118 (top left), 121 (top right), 122 (top), 123 (bottom), 125, 126, 128, 133 (all), 135 (top), 141 (both), 143, 148, 152 (all), 157 (right), 158 (all), 159, 160 (top left, right), 161 (bottom), 164, 176 (both), 182, 217 (both), 218*

Donald Danforth Plant Science Center: *288, 289 (top left)*

Donn Rubin, BioSTL: *287 (top)*

Temple Shaare Emeth/Rabbi Jeffrey Stiffman: *18 (top)*

Library of Congress, Geography and Map Division: *Front cover (top right), 24 (right), 29*

Wells Fargo: *3 (left), 8, 23*

West End Word: *5, 149, 177 (top), 178 (bottom left), 198, 204, 205, 208, 209 (both), 226 (right), 256 (top)*

West End Word **(photographer, Diana Linsley):** *199*

Jeff Fister of Virginia Publishing: *202*

Washington University Department of Special Collections: *4 (left), 14, 26 (bottom right), 54 (top), 60 (bottom), 72 (both), 73, 74 (all)*

Washington University in St. Louis Photos: *Back cover (bottom far left, bottom middle left, bottom center, bottom middle right), 6 (left, right), 257, 258, 262 (right), 268 (bottom), 269, 270 (right) 273 (top), 274, 275 (both), 279 (both), 284, 285 (right), 286, 287 (bottom left), 299, 300 (both), 301 (both)*

***Washington University Magazine*, Spring 1975:** *212 (both)*

***Washington University Magazine*, Fall 1996:** *221*

***Washington University Record*, December 8, 2000:** *224 (bottom)*

World Chess Hall of Fame: *6 (middle), 262 (top left, bottom left)*

Saint Louis Zoo: *62 (right), 63, 160 (bottom left)*

Archives of the Diocese of Missouri: *100 (top), 101*

Archives of Trinity Church, St. Louis: *100 (bottom)*

Central West End Association: *Back cover (top), 210 (bottom), 244 (top), 270 (left), 273 (bottom), 275 (right)*

Forest Park Forever: *264 (left), 265 (top left, bottom left), 267 (middle left), 299 (top)*

Forest Park Forever (photographer, Calla Massman): *Front cover (middle right), 267 (top left, bottom, right), 271 (both)*

Forest Park Forever (photographer, Randy Allen): *Back cover (bottom far right), 266*

Forest Park Forever (photographer, Julie Anderson): *270 (left)*

Christner, Inc.: *264 (right), 265 (top)*

The Mary Institute Archives: *93 (both)*

St. Louis Post-Dispatch: *19 (bottom), 36 (bottom), 40 (both), 55 (top), 67 (both), 88, 89 (bottom), 94 (bottom), 95 (middle, bottom), 99 (right), 100 (middle), 104 (bottom), 105 (bottom left, bottom right), 106 (left), 114 (bottom), 115, 116, 117 (both), 122 (bottom), 123 (top), 124, 127 (both), 130 (right), 131, 132 (both), 135 (bottom), 137 (both), 138 (both), 139, 145, 146 (top), 149 (all), 150, 151 (all), 153 (both), 154, 155 (top), 156 (both), 157 (left), 166 (bottom, inset), 167 (both), 168, 171, 173, 174 (both), 175 (top), 177 (bottom), 178 (top right, top left, bottom right), 179 (both), 180, 183, 184 (both), 186 (top), 187 (all), 188, 189, 191, 193 (both), 194 (both), 195 (both), 196, 197 (all), 203 (both), 207, 210 (both), 211 (both), 224 (top), 239 (top), 241, 242, 243 (top), 246 (both), 249, 250 (both), 252 (top), 253 (both), 254 (all), 255, 256 (bottom), 259 (both), 260, 261 (both), 263, 268 (top), 272, 277 (top), 282 (both), 283 (left), 285 (left), 295 (both), 297 (both)*

The St. Louis Republic: *19 (top), 86 (bottom right), 97 (bottom)*

St. Louis Star and Times: *94 (top), 95 (top), 103, 107 (middle), 118 (bottom left, top right), 119 (both), 120 (bottom), 130 (left), 142 (bottom), 146 (bottom), 155 (bottom)*

St. Louis Globe-Democrat: *234, 235 (all)*

Courtesy of Cortex (photographer Romondo Davis): *280, 296*

Courtesy of Cortex: *7 (bottom), 287 (right), 289 (bottom) 293*

Courtesy of Post-Polio Health International: *252 (bottom)*

Rendering © and courtesy Studio Gang: *283 (right)*

Second Presbyterian Church/Rev. Donald Cochran: *Front cover (middle left)*